Best Wish

& Bless !

God

Brian Tracy

Today's World

Poetry: Based on Real Life

by
Brian Tusing

Bloomington, IN  Milton Keynes, UK

authorHOUSE®

AuthorHouse™
1663 Liberty Drive, Suite 200
Bloomington, IN 47403
www.authorhouse.com
Phone: 1-800-839-8640

AuthorHouse™ UK Ltd.
500 Avebury Boulevard
Central Milton Keynes, MK9 2BE
www.authorhouse.co.uk
Phone: 08001974150

First published by AuthorHouse 12/26/2006

ISBN: 978-1-4259-6556-3 (sc)

Printed in the United States of America
Bloomington, Indiana

This book is printed on acid-free paper.

ACKNOWLEDGEMENTS

Special thanks to:

God Almighty; whom without, none of this would be possible.

My family for their love and support, The History Channel, National Geographic, Dan & Mary Ann Jones, Michael Outland Jr., Larry Fitch, Robert Smith...

And to the readers for their time.

Contents

CHAPTER I – FAMILY

BEFORE THE KNOT IS TIED

Look deep in my eyes
Tell me what you see
Mixed feelings about a marriage
That someday may come to be

Should I tie the knot,
Or leave the strings undone?
It's hard to part with what I've always had
That being 31 years of fun.

I want to do what is best
But I know not what to choose
There is a sensation of love in the air
That I do not want to lose.

There is still something I long for
Something I've never had
To be hitched with a gorgeous babe
For the things I've experienced in life, I am glad.

Sometimes life is so unfair
You wonder which way to go
When this happens from time to time
Don't lose grip and take things slow.

MY WIFE

A lady in my life with the profession as a nurse
Who saved me from army life that could have been worse
Talking on the internet I asked for her name
I'll answer your question but ask you the same

After the army I moved into her home
I had my white car without any chrome
I came and I went every day for a year
Feeling that sometime the wedding day was near

We got along great, no arguments or fights
I laid out my rules and explained to her my rights
All before marriage there were the growing pains
Not yet 'hitched' we were in 2 separate lanes

One day in the kitchen she was cooking something
I thought this time was good as any, so I offered a ring
The offer was accepted; her answer is 'I do'
Now the date is planned when I will marry you

Having a companion by my side, life got better every day
I had my fun being single but didn't want to die that way
The big day was upon us, both of us being afraid
Of what the future holds for us, I hope she makes the grade!

The wedding day is over, the two of us become one
Thinking about baby names, she's going to have a son
A rocky road to birth, with a child we are blessed
The 4lb. little baby, daddy wishes for him the best

Now we are parents with love growing every day
With baby being little he doesn't have much to say
Looking out for the little one, the parents' love is true
I'm glad things turned out the way they did.
To my family: I love you!!

BABY

I was in the army, now I'm married
In the future there may be a baby, by mother it will be
carried.
These words are written in the dark, looking at the stars
My mind is on the future goals; all old ones are mental scars

Now that I'm hitched, a little one is planned
He will arrive in the later part of the year; His entrance will
be grand
We wish for a healthy baby, good in every way
Who knows when he will come, will it be night or will it be
day

Sitting in the garage, writing ever word
When he's born there will be cries, these sounds will be heard

The wife is going easy; she takes it day by day
One of these days it will happen soon, for the loss of pain she
will pray
When the little one comes, new trends will need to be set
While bringing baby forward, Mother will begin to sweat

Once baby gets here I hope we know what to do
It doesn't matter what happens, Parents' love will be true
After all of the excitement the baby will sleep
We will be cautious of sound, not to make a peep.

JACOB

Jacob arrived in the month of September
His birthday will be easy to remember
He was a little tiny baby; weight of 4 pounds (13oz.)
Mom was knocked out, she heard only whimpering sounds.

He used to be a tired baby, sleeping every hour
Now he has a new diet, new food to devour.
Little Jacob is making sounds, learning how to talk
When he is held, he wants to learn how to walk.

He wakes every morning with a smile on his face
Before every meal he will learn to say Grace.
Baby makes us smile, always having fun
Trying to capture the moments, the video cam will run.

Up during the night, many times he cries
A baby will change your life when you look into their eyes.
Now he has pain, receiving his first tooth in July
Soon will be new groceries, new food to buy.

Now Jacob walks, he is all over the floor
He will let you know when he wants no more
He had a fever, his skin felt hot to the touch
He runs around the house and doesn't need a crutch.

His brain is growing, getting smarter day by day
I hope he is successful in life, his dues he will have to pay.
Like everyone else, he will have to do the same
Who knows what he'll want? A family, fortune, or fame?

For now he will live the life of a child
We will try to take it easy so he won't end up wild.

A CHILD GROWING

One day about 9 months away
Little Jacob will have a sister or brother
Now he will have a person with which to play
That will be brought to him by his mother

They will not be raised like many of today's youth
Dressed in rags, wearing pants that hang to the knees
They will be taught to always tell the truth
And learn words like 'Thank you' and 'Please'

At 2 years of age he's into every little thing
Never seeming to have any satisfaction
Screaming at the birds, he makes the ears ring
Yelling through the house just for a reaction

Now able to walk, he must learn to speak
Gaining knowledge will never stop
Now potty training, the bathroom he must seek
And next, it's the pacifier he has to drop

It's fun to watch children grow
Passing time is filled with joy
Growing older he will soon know
That mommy & daddy love their little boy

ANOTHER BABY

Mommy has a test of her blood
It shows new life on the way
She comes home and tells me its positive
For a moment, I know not what to say

Brother, sister, & family are called
Everyone is given the news
Congratulations come from all sides
The first born enters his " Terrible 2's "

The pregnancy term is 9 months
Time for baby's arrival at planet earth
Boy or girl, a healthy little one is prayed for
Around the month of April will be baby's birth

Loving parents are happy
This will be her second child to bare
With the same expectations as the first born
Letting them know that mommy and daddy care.

A CALL FROM BROTHER

Just last week came a call from brother
After such a long time, still had nothing to say
With a trashy mouth I didn't want to hear
I see his way of thinking is in disarray

He says he's tired of his way of living
Not wanting the same old thing
Deep inside I think he longs to change
Maybe being afraid of what the future will bring

Acting like a bully to his little brother as a child
A close family relationship we never had
Now we're all grown, by me he is forgiven
Dependant of chemicals for a long time has made his brain mad

The Bible was suggested to him
He thinks there is nothing after death
I hope one day he opens his eyes to his future
Before he winds up breathing his last breath

He speaks of not wanting a wife and children
I tell him "Find the right one & life could be a blast"
That's alright if he wants to be on his own
It could be more fun if he changes his life from ways of his past

Tired of being around blue uniforms 24/7
Starting to get fed-up with his way of living
Getting rid of the strife he can still get to Heaven
Through mercy, love, and the power of prayer, God is
forgiving

Hoping he changes his life
Before the time is too late
Praying at the end of his days
He's able to pass through Heaven's Gate.

JACOB 2 YEARS OLD

Having a birthday in the month of September
Little Jacob is now 2 years old
It amazes parents, the things he can remember
A toddler full of energy but does what he is told

He would rather play with pots & pans than his toys
Getting excited when he sees the birds
Having an energy rush, making lots of noise
He's now at the point of uttering words

His left thumb doesn't fully bend
Moving slightly more than half of its range
Doctors operate on the bone, the cut they will mend
Looking at his hand, he knows something is strange

Sometimes it seems he's too smart for his britches
Doing something wrong, he knows he'll get caught
On his little thumb he now has 2 stitches
Saying and doing things that he was never taught

With a blessing from above will come a 2nd child
Fulfilling our family plan in the coming spring
Notifying family & friends, the telephone will be dialed
We'll have to see what the future will bring.

BABY'S ULTRASOUND

On November 11th, to the doctor's office we go
To have an ultrasound procedure done
The doctor checks the heart and blood flow
Parents ask; is it a daughter or a son?

Doc checks all organs to make sure they are there
Counting 10 fingers and 10 toes
As he continues to look, at the monitor we stare
While he measures the head, face, and nose

Measuring the whole body and many different bones
Checking out every angle and curl
Looking between the legs for 2 little 'stones'
He sees nothing and says it must be a girl

The hospital gave us some pictures
To post in the baby's book
In the pages they will be permanent fixtures
Before birth, baby can see how she used to look.

A NEW ADDITION

Mother is pregnant with her 2nd child
After this one, no more are planned
At 28 weeks, time is drawing closer
Soon the birth of a girl will be at hand

Watching her belly, she sees the baby kick
Baby gets comfortable while stretching inside
In the month of April will be her time to emerge
Exiting the womb to a new world outside

Mommy's wish for children is granted
Having 1 little girl and 1 baby boy
Coming home from the hospital with a newborn
It seems this year mommy has a new toy

Daughter's birth has been long awaited
A possible name selected being Brianna Rene
Made from half of mom and half of dad
A part of her parents she will have 'til her last day

Having a brother 2 years older
The little boy now has a playmate
Hopefully teaching baby sister what not to do
Living in their own little world that they create.

BLESSED WITH 2ND CHILD

Birth of the baby girl is about a week away
In different months, siblings were to share the same birthday
30 was the magic number, 2&1/2 years set them apart
Now there will be 2 children to shop for at Wal-Mart

Mommy experiences many of the same things as before
Soon 2 children will greet her at the door
Similar to her brother, at birth she'll be low in weight
Due to conditions of mother while in this pregnant state

In the very near future, the family will be complete
With 1 boy & 1 girl, the parents have received their treat
The desired family came to be with 2 gifts from above
Offspring of the opposite sex that mommy & daddy love

Mom & dad wonder, will she look like her brother?
Given traits and genes passed by father and mother
The main concern is good health for baby is desired
2 little miracles from a womb that was divinely inspired.

THE 2ND BABY BORN

After the 1st little one, a 2nd is planned
The gift of a baby girl is desired
With ultra-sound technology the fetus is scanned
Looking at the image', our hope was inspired

The doctor informed us what the sex should be
A healthy infant is the parents' main concern
Another addition is made to the family tree
As pregnancy advances the baby begins to turn

Months go by as the time draws near
In the season of spring the baby will arrive
Experiencing delivery, in my eye there's a tear
Hearing the cries & whimpers is a sign she's alive

Parents are filled with joy for the new baby
Prayers were answered for this family of 3
Question of a 3rd child was a big 'maybe'
This little girl acquiring the nickname of 'Bri'

After her 1st year, Brianna is doing well
Parents love her just as much as the boy
The happiness of new life causes emotions to swell
A happy family completed with the new bundle of joy.

We love you 'Bri-Bri'…XOXO

CHAPTER II – GOVT & POLITICAL

TERRORISTS

What is wrong with the world today?
Terrorists; dressed in clothes & hoods of black
They are hidden in every part of the world
But are based in the Middle East & Iraq

Osama Bin Laden is the network leader
Then there are tyrants like Saddam Hussein
They support murder & persecution of the innocent
The fear factor keeps them powerful in their reign

Pictures circulate throughout the media
American soldiers abusing prisoners of war
A decapitated American contractor on TV
Is a victim in Iraq to 'even their score'

The acts of 9-11-01 are the reason we're in the east
The terrorists should learn to be a free nation
The resolve of the U.S. will not break
We will be in this turmoil for the duration

Politics plays a large role
In the terrorists empires that are made
One day; probably the end of the world
Is when all their problems and antics will fade.

AMERICAN GOVT.

The govt. needs revenue
The money will come from tax /
When you get old & can no longer pay
There's nothing left but getting 'The Axe'

We elect officials into office
They seldom do their job
They vote their own raises & terms
The poor, struggling public are the people they rob

In the words of Gov. Jesse Ventura
'There is only 1 tax that is just'
That is a tax of 'Consumption'
A politician is someone you can't trust

The lawmakers are undependable
Without their ego they would bust
The greedy officials want the almighty dollar
With words that are printed 'In God We Trust'

The people are the ones to suffer
Sacrificing for every dime
Many feel the burden of taxation,
Should be declared a federal crime.

$ MONEY $

Money is the root of all evil today
It's the main thing that makes the world go 'round
The rich are getting richer, with much on their tray
They only think of one thing, that 'JINGLING' sound.

People in Pro- sports are some of the highest paid
Multi-million dollar contracts in ink are signed
Do they really need all the money that is made?
The rich make big ' Donations' to act like they are kind

The lottery for instance, most of the winnings go to one
Why not make the number of winners more?
With minds filled with greed they take the money & run
With more winners spending, the economy would soar.

Now onto the legislature, corrupted by what they get
Spending taxpayer dollars with no apparent goal
In this ground the fiscal structure is set
The govt. has made it's bed, $3 trillion in the hole.

You can't take it with you when you go to the grave
It's the power & greed that changes thinking in the brain
It's the middle class & the poor who are unable to save
Spending & greed is out of control, like a runaway train.

ELECTION DAY

Coming in the month of November
Every 4th year the possibility of a new member
The office of the presidency has a seat to fill
The winning candidates' new home is on Capitol Hill

Democrat or Republican, they desire every vote
The outgoing president is the one we will demote
Known as Election Day is when their time will come
Now out of office, they go back to where they're from

Traveling the country on the road of the campaign
Speaking to the masses, the lost vote they wish to gain
The campaign ads are on every television show
As the politicians debate, they go toe to toe

Uncovering the dirt, about the other, stories are told
More like a popularity contest, the people are polled
The poll results show where the people stand
On the issues of this country and every other land

To gain each vote is their objective for the day
Once in office, they do half of what they say
Each one thinks he can do better than the last
On the deciding day is when all votes will be cast

After all votes are counted, a winner will be crowned
Making his 1st speech, in the White House he can be found
The big day is over, the next in 4 more years
Executing the office, he will be judged by his peers.

THE U.S. FLAG

A banner decorated with stripes & stars
The color of horizontal red & white bars
Hanging on a pole, in the wind it will fly
When a soldier's life is over, on the casket it will lie

It symbolizes a country that is free
Giving it's citizens life & liberty
She flies at many buildings, stadiums, and schools
The blood given for her reason could fill many pools

This piece of linen is called the U.S. Flag
Foreigners set it ablaze like some sort of dirty rag
They like to watch the red, white, & blue turn black
Terrorists and radical militants who are in Iraq

The stars & stripes has flown for over 200 years
After the national anthem plays, there will be cheers
Freedom, liberty, & strength are what she represents
The ones who hate it most are the Arabs in their tents

Old Glory's birthday is on the 4th of July
Firecrackers & bombs explode in the night sky
Everywhere you look, you will see one every day
The symbols the flag stands for will never go away

For a free society she still stands
A country built by many working hands
For a country of democracy, this banner leads the way
It will fly on the erected pole forever and a day.

CURRENT EVENTS 2004

These are the issues of the world today
A marriage ban of people that are gay
Marriage happens with a girl and a boy
Not to be used as a homosexual toy

In the beginning God created Adam & Eve
In the new millennium man created Adam & Steve
It would be nice if immorality didn't exist
Leaders in other countries rule with an iron fist

Mt. St. Helens rumbled last week
Scientists say soon it may blow its peak
In the year 2004 there is a war in Iraq
Started in New York with a World Trade Center attack

In our pledge and our money, they want to remove God
The evil things in this world, don't they seem odd?
The Bible in front of the court, they want it gone
The judicial system's ruling? They have until dawn

Taking away religion, the world needs more of the savior
Even 2000 years ago, people still had bad behavior
Searching for aliens & UFO's and anything that's strange
The twisted world we live in seems will never change

The family concept in this country is a shock
A divorce rate of 50% and children born out of wedlock
Seasons are changing because the ozone is shrinking
It seems logic has disappeared, what are people thinking?

In the govt. budget there is a huge debt
Arguing over taxes, other issues they forget
Now there is a shortage of the flu vaccine
People thirst in poverty because the water isn't clean

Prescription drugs are getting harder to obtain
For the sick, elderly, and people who have pain
The price of crude oil goes higher day by day
Society feels the crunch at the gas pumps where they pay

Some people don't believe what the future has in store
There are some that think the end will be the 3rd world war
Those who experience the end, their jaws will hit the floor
There will come a day when the world is no more.

OVERSTEPPING THE BOUNDARIES

Why mess with the stem cell?
To create the cell, life must be destroyed
What happened to the morals of mankind?
With new knowledge, scientists are overjoyed

Society is overstepping its boundaries
Toying with things that we should not
Now they want to control the weather
To regulate things that are cold and hot

Why not let nature take its course?
Deal with the things that come your way
Man is getting too smart for his own good
Eventually, this world is going to go away

The wheels of time have been set in motion
The world is reaching its last days
Catastrophic disasters cause lots of commotion
Mankind should turn from his evil ways

Stem cell work and aborted pregnancies
No matter how looked upon, it is killing
The human race will destruct itself
Started by the human blood that is spilling

Searching for the answer to every question
Some things would be better off if left alone
The curious beings we are, we will always search
It may be a nuclear blast that cooks every human bone

Scientists turn to genetic engineering
Trying to create the perfect animal or plant
Man thinks he's so intelligent but really is not
Striving to control some things that he can't

Mankind trying to control his own destiny
The divine word states the world will cease to exist
What will man decide to tinker with next?
With everything we've done, what's next on the list?

THE S.A.CARTELS

High in the mountains of South America
Crops are grown of coffee and coca
The coffee bean is ground for a beverage
With the coca plant, cartels gain leverage

These products are the country's main export
The byproduct of coca is transported with an escort
The processed leaves yield the powder of cocaine
Smuggled into the U.S. by boat, truck, or plane

Cartels are financed with the money from the drugs
The main boss gets rich with the help of hired thugs
Deep in the jungle is where the processing takes place
Almost busted, the workers are gone without a trace

Eliminating any intruder in the blink of an eye
To protect the secret business, some are willing to die
Bolivia, Peru, and Colombia is the primary area of operation
In the hills of these countries can be found the 'coke
plantation'

Law enforcement agents destroy a field of crops
The trafficking of the illegal substance never stops
Plants set ablaze in what is called a 'controlled burn'
The field has a new location; it seems the cartels never learn.

IRAQ WAR

Starting in Kuwait, then moving northward
The objective is the city of Baghdad
A long journey through what was once Persia
Conditions during the advancement are getting bad

A maintenance unit comes under fire
Enemy units take U.S. hostages away
The future is unforeseeable for this group of soldiers
They can only hope they live to see another day

Later in time, after the war has begun
The hostages are rescued by U.S. Special Forces
As war and fighting intensify day by day
Along the roadside are dead Iraqi corpses

Waiting for the arrival of U.S. forces
In the capitol is the Elite Republican Guard
As Saddam Hussein awaits the onslaught
This group of soldiers are his 'Trump Card'

The Republican Guard is not able to hold ground
At the Baghdad Airport they face defeat
As the 'Shock and Awl' takes its effect
The only option is for the Husseins to retreat

Seizing every palace and key building
Saddam and his sons run and hide
Eventually in the city of Tikrit
A 'spider hole' is found with Saddam inside

After the Baath Party is toppled
The loyalists still stand and fight
Rounding up fugitives from the 'deck of cards'
Terrorist strongholds are pounded day and night

Insurgents persist to disrupt operations
U.S. soldiers battle through pain and strife
Iraqi liberation is one of the main goals
As some U.S. soldiers pay the ultimate price with their life

Terrorists and criminals are pursued
Throughout the city and in every direction
A free Iraq is desired by many individuals
On the present path they will hold their 1st election

Giving control back to the Iraqi people
The U.S. purpose is not to occupy
Making Iraq free from oppression
Showing them a new way on which to rely.

PROBLEMS FACING THE U.S.

Open up your eyes and your mind
Take a look at the world around you
Disasters taking place of every kind
There are those today that don't have a clue

The govt. has a blind eye to illegal immigration
Having difficulty sealing the border in the south
By the thousands they come into this nation
No plan presented by Congressional mouth

Injustice & incompetence occurring in the court
Murderers and criminals are sometimes let go
Officials take action with failure to report
The way things are handled; problems will only grow

Kids now are shooting guns within the schools
A flaw in the system causes judges to be killed
These actions eliminated with the enforcement of rules
No room for law-breakers 'cause the prisons are overfilled

Scandals uncovered with the big company's chief
Celebrities involved in a high profile lawsuit
It seems these days that everyone is a thief
Cheating when they can to obtain their loot

The future is determined by decisions made now
Watch the level of corruption as it climbs
People must change but they don't know how
These are a few of the 'Signs Of The Times'

CHAPTER III – NATURE

OUR UNIVERSE

In the sky is the sun burning bright
Providing year 'round heat and light
When the sun sets there are colors that change
In the evening hours the sky will rearrange

The blue of day turns to black at night
At this time the moon and stars shine bright
Stars' distance from the earth is measured in light years
The earth rotates slowly as the next day nears

In our solar system there are 9 planets in all
The first and last planets are the ones that are small
In the middle they get bigger with Jupiter at the top
Once past Pluto the space doesn't stop

A streak in the night sky signals a shooting star
Also called a comet, I've seen one from my car
The heavens start to brighten as the sun starts to rise
Never stare into the sun, it burns the retina in the eyes

Man has built rockets to travel to the moon
Then came the space shuttle not a moment too soon
A reusable spacecraft that lands like a plane
The inventions man dreams up starts in the brain

The blue sky is blocked by clouds that are thick
A change in the weather could make the roads slick
Away with the clouds and the blue returns
Even in the dark of night the sun still burns

Distance from the sun to earth is 93 million miles
Glasses made for the sun's bright light come in many styles
Scientists use telescopes to look beyond the stars
Searching for life and water we send a probe to Mars

Once the day breaks then the night falls
People sleeping in houses, horses in their stalls
Sun returns in the morning, the darkness is called night
Constellations make figures when the sun is out of sight

Making pictures of the Zodiac in the dark sky
The darkest reaches of space can't be seen with the eye
The telescope helps but still can see no end
Will the sun ever stop shining? The experts can't say when

How was the universe created? Nobody seems to know
The first chapters of Genesis will make the scientists a pro
Why do they keep searching? The answer is in their head
Learning much more about life, the 'Good Book' should be read.

THE THUNDERSTORM

Looking from the driveway, approaching clouds are dark
Time for children to go home and stay away from the park
The swirling sky is a mix of white, gray, and black
The lightning and the thunder are signs of nature's attack

The super-cell is violent with very unstable air
The storm spawns tornadoes, more than 1 is not rare
The wind funnel touches down leveling everything in sight
A house in the path of this monster is fighting a losing fight

The strong thunderstorm produces hail and rain
Tornadoes produce destruction, misery, and pain
The cloudburst beats down filling every drain
The activity in a storm is anything but mundane

The storm gains strength from the rising daytime heat
When too much rain falls there is flooding in the street
Clouds are many miles wide, the cell is seldom small
The air mass moves at different speeds, sometimes it will stall

In the season of spring is when the most tornadoes are born
Nothing is left standing, buildings and trees are torn
When you look into the sky and see dark clouds on the way
Don't be sad if you like the sun, it will be back another day

When the big storm comes it brings wind, rain, and hail
The funnel drops from the sky and leaves chaos in its trail
Thunderstorms are a force of nature, nothing man can control
The destruction it leaves behind will surely take its toll.

THE OCEANS' IMPACT

Water covers about 75% of the earth
In the depths many fish can be found
Influencing climate around the world
The deepest trenches can be 2 miles down

The oceans separate diverse ways of life
And the masses of land where they dwell
When the weather gets nasty the seas can be a weapon
Wrecking waterfront businesses so they can no longer sell

The wrath of the ocean creates a very high tide
Water floods the surrounding land
Washing away any man made structure
While eroding the beaches of sand

In a circular arrangement of clouds
The ocean gives the hurricane its power
Unloading high winds and flooding waters
That pounds the coast hour after hour

Oceans have a great impact on civilization
Supporting species of every kind
Without the water the world would be a desert
The only planet with water is the way earth was designed

The marine world can be used for recreation
For boating, fishing, and the beaches
When wading or swimming in fresh water lakes
Beware of the blood-sucking leeches

Respect the ocean for the power it possesses
But beware of its violent wrath
Evacuate when there is bad weather on the way
Soon, the towns around you will receive natures' bath.

RAINY DAY

A gloomy day, the rain pouring down
Clouds are dark, blocking out the blue sky
Everything is soaked all around town
In a day or two, everything will be dry

The precipitation cleans the streets
The water fills up the drying lake
To plants and animals it brings natures' treats
In the winter when frozen, it will fall as a flake

Rain helps vegetation to stay alive
Anything not watertight will begin to leak
Without water on earth, nothing would survive
That would make chances of life very weak

Some rain is good, more than enough is not
It floods the land, the ground you can't see
Breeding the bugs that campers want to swat
Rain storms get water and strength from the sea

Having a BBQ, friends & family you can invite
After the water falls from the sky above
Darkness of the clouds gives way to the light
Good weather approaches that most people love

Watching falling water, children think it's neat
When the rain is gone is when the cycle will repeat.

THE UNDISCOVERED WONDER

Hidden in the forest, away in the trees
The man-like beast covered with hair
Reported through folklore over generations
Is there an undiscovered species really out there?

Hundreds of footprints are collected
Many eyewitness stories are told
Scientific researchers even find hair samples
Through all temperatures and climates, hot and cold

Over the years movies and videos are taken
The need for evidence is met
The remains of a dead body have not been found
Nobody has been able to capture one yet

The American Indians call it Sasquatch
In the Himalayas they call it the yeti
How can it be elusive for such a long time?
Looking for answers, science is ready

Others see something in the Loch
An animal of some kind in the Scotland lake
There are those that believe and ones who are optimistic
Until conclusive evidence is found, they will think its fake

Sightings come the mountains, lakes & the Pacific Northwest
Of objects that people can't comprehend
Telling their stories and searching for explanations
For now all clues and evidence is reaching a dead end.

NATURAL PARKS

Rolling hills with a quiet meadow
See the sun rise and set over tops of trees
Like something out of a wilderness movie
You can find peace and solitude with the animals & the bees

The natural habitat is shrinking
Trees are disappearing every day
If humans don't respect Mother Nature,
All wildlife will have no place to stay

There are places around called national parks
Here, the bears & wolves will find a home
In these refuges the trees will always stand
On this land all wild animals can roam

In Wyoming is a park called Yellowstone
One of the biggest in the United States
You can see 'Old Faithful' and big mountains here
It's a place the lumber industry hates

In California there are the giant redwoods
Home to many critters and many birds
Leave nature as it was intended to be
There is a message for the loggers in these words

Much work is needed for the goals that are set
From now until the duration
When you're off from work & need somewhere to go
Visit with Mother Nature outdoors; take a vacation.

WILDERNESS TIME

Tall green pines reflect off the lake
Mountains in the background topped with white caps
In an empty campground is a left over steak
On a windy day a few trees collapse

A stream nearby; the sound of water trickling
The water is cool and crystal clear
A couple on the road are cross-country bicycling
Sounds like a commercial in Colorado for beer

A log cabin in the forest; feel the cool morning air
Wild animals are foraging for food
Herds of bison and deer roam without a care
Trash around the parks; people littering are rude

A spring spills from the rocks of a mountainous domain
Trails of caverns are cut into the hill
In the distance you can hear a faint sound of a train
No disturbance in the weather, everything is still

The river goes for miles as the water flows free
The beavers are busy building a dam
The beauty of the wilderness is something to see
Roaming the mountainside is where you'll find a ram

The sun comes up; it is now the break of day
The meadow is full of wildflowers with dew
Rain arrives, as the sky turns gray
On a cliff of the Grand Canyon is an awesome view

A serene time in life, lose yourself in peace and quiet
No worries; let your mind wander free
Starting a fire, you caught a fish, now you fry it
Forget about all troubles, enjoy yourself is the key.

VOLCANO

Magma spews from the center of the earth
This molten liquid gives the volcano it's birth
Eruptions shoot out fire and ash
Coming to the surface through the land's gash

Islands form in the middle of the sea
Lava on land burns down every tree
Lava is molten rock, which comes from the ground
In the trail of the flow, only rock can be found

Volcanoes in Hawaii are still active today
People in near-by towns will want to run away
The sleeping giants are violent when awake
When the lava starts to flow, lives are at stake

Magma in the oceans cools at a rapid pace
After the eruption life disappears without a trace
A hole in the mountain is known as the crater
If I'm ever in the path, I'll have to see ya later!

LOST IN THE DESERT

Lost in the desert; Left for the 3rd time in 2 days
I look to the mountains & see a hot haze
The land goes on and on, where anything can roam
I'm tired of being in the sandbox; I wanna go home!

This place is so dead, there's not much here
I never asked to come to this hole; I wish my home were near!
I could start walking but there's no place to go
Nothing can survive here; it's only the weeds that grow.

For one week now I've not seen one cloud
Sometimes I want to scream out loud.
If you listen closely only silence will be heard
Stay in the sun too long and your vision will be blurred.

Here with my truck, I stand alone
This is getting to be a habit I do not condone!
Waiting for some help, nobody comes my way
There's nothing I can do; here I must stay.

It's getting darker; nightfall is coming soon
You may hear a coyote or 2 barking at the moon.
Soon I will sleep until the morning
Then it will get hot as hell without warning.

I listen to the radio; that's how I spend my day
Hoping for a solution, there has to be a way
I guess I'll go wait some more & see if someone will show
If they don't, I may be gone from this world tomorrow.

CLOUDS

The clouds are flying today
I'm in a land far away
There are many different shades in the sky
Sometimes I look at them and wonder why

The birds are flying high in the air
The clouds are bright like Snow White's hair
They sometimes come and darken the day
That usually means rain is on the way

They're big, white, and puffy like cotton
They add life to the sky and bad dreams are forgotten
Some soar high and some hang low
Today I see many that are as white as snow

They cover up the blue, they run into the hill
I see this sometimes from my bedroom windowsill
They hang over the trees, and like them they make shade
When they cover up the sun, cooler temperatures are made

Today I'm working beneath them; the sun begins to disappear
I know the sun will be seen again, so for this I have no fear
I guess I'll close for now and finish off the day
If there's no sun in your life, soon you'll catch a ray.

AQUATIC FOOD CHAIN

Most of the fish the sea have scales
Moving along the bottom making sandy trails
Creatures with enemies try to hide
Finding holes or caves to go inside

Having their place within the food chain
One fish's loss is another one's gain
The bigger fish are closer to the top
The scavengers on the bottom eating all the slop

Swimming most of the time, it seems they never sleep
Feeding on fish and other creatures of the deep
The shark is probably the largest predator in the sea
Attacking swimmers at the beach which could be you or me

They don't want or like the taste of human flesh
Sometimes their life is ended within the fisherman's mesh
In the depths of the water is where they like to hide
Most people like their fish oven baked or fried

The aquatic world provides food for the earth
For the species to survive it's necessary they give birth
Animals serve their purpose, being eaten for their meat
Through death & reproduction, the food chain is complete.

CATASRTOPHIC TSUNAMI 2004

At the bottom of the Indian Ocean
6 miles deep within the ground
Tectonic plates cause a 9.0 quake
Sending 20 to 30 ft. waves to many countries around

Traveling hundreds of miles per hour
The massive waves approach the coast
On this day, people that are near the beach
Try to hang on to any tree or post

The wall of water slams into the mainland
The disaster comes without a sound
Washing away everything in sight
In several countries, there were many dead found

People were swallowed up by the ocean
More than 250,000 humans lost their lives
A catastrophic event that they never saw coming
The people were sons, daughters, husbands, & wives

Vibrations start to shake the ocean floor
Like a pebble in a puddle, the water begins to move
The energy spreads in every direction
Showing the power Mother Nature doesn't need to prove

One natural disaster after another
Is this humanity's punishment for all its crimes?
Many think we are near the end of earth's days
With catastrophic events like this as signs of the times.

FULL MOON

Shining bright is a full moon in the sky
Emerging are nocturnal creatures that crawl and fly
A force of nature with influence on various things
Having an impact on humans, with the strange behavior it
brings

Earth is affected by the moon's gravity
Controlling the tides and the ocean's activity
Strange things occur when the moon is full
Tides rise and crime stats increase due to the gravitational
pull

In the dark wilderness the moon provides light
Emanating its brightest on a clear, cloud free night
Getting its light from a reflection of the sun
Some planets have many moons but the earth has only one

Full of craters, the surface looks like swiss cheese
Dark parts of the surface are known as waterless seas
The main crater called Tycho can be seen with the naked eye
When the full moon shines bright in the nighttime sky.

EARTH THREATENING ELEMENTS

If & when the super volcano erupts
The pyroclastic flows will go on for miles
Prevailing winds can blow debris up to 1000 miles away
Burying entire cities in soot and ash piles

Under Yellowstone Park sits one of these giants
It could erupt within the next 100,000 years
The odds of this happening is about 1 in 20,000
But the possibility is what human civilization fears

Exploding with the power of every atomic bomb on earth
Detonating at the same time and in the same place
Making the Mt. St. Helens eruption look weak
Another earth shattering object lurks in space

A catastrophic impact of an asteroid and the earth
Is the next disaster that poses a threat
Located in the Arizona desert is a 1-mile crater
Showing us signs that we can never forget

Natural disasters are occurring more frequently
It seems every month or 2; something else is swept away
Patterns are rearranging in this ever-changing world
Leaving behind death, destruction, and decay

Ice, fire, water, and space are the elements
Will it be a flood, ice age, inferno, or asteroid?
The forces of nature cannot be controlled
Earth's final destruction is something mankind can't avoid.

CHAPTER IV – HISTORY

MICHEL DE NOSTRADAME
(Nostradamus)

Sitting in his study room in his home country of France
Preparing for a night of writing, his mind is in a trance
Looking into the pot, he sees things he can't explain
Jotting down on paper the thoughts that are in his brain

Little did he know he was seeing future events
The ideas he had, to him made little sense
Working as a physician, he helped his sisters and brothers
The verses in the writings were a warning to all others

He predicted his exhumation with a medallion around his neck
Writing of the man-made mountains, where 2 planes were to wreck
Telling of Nazi Germany, communism, and American presidents
Suggesting future events, his centuries & quatrains are the evidence

Many of his writings have already come true
There are many more that need studying, more that are new
There are always the doubters, the ones that see not the light
He only wrote what he saw, he had no idea he would be right.

CIVIL WAR FLAG

A red colored banner with an 'X' on it's face
Inside of the 'X' are stars in this space
The rebel flag is a sign of the south
A brother killing brother leaves a bad taste in their mouth

The confederate flag was flown in the Civil War
The battles between countrymen was very hardcore
When Lincoln was president he freed every slave
A noble effort on his part, their future he did save

In the capital of Georgia it is still flown today
Some disapprove of its symbol; others think its okay
A little piece of history etched in the annals of time
Trading in the gray uniforms for as little as a dime

The money had more worth then, they didn't need that much
Many soldiers lost their lives; to walk some needed a crutch
This flag saw many battles of gray against the blue
Fought in Maryland, Virginia, and Pennsylvania too

The rebel flag was born when this country was in its youth
The infamous triggerman of Lincoln was named John Wilkes
Booth
These battles are now history; the country wants no more
What is the fate of this country? Let's see what time has in store

Fellow Americans buried the hatchet; they tried to make amends
Others should look at this free country and see the message it
sends
Nobody likes war in their country when the opponents are
their own
In a time like our Civil War when the confederate flag was flown.

HISTORY HUNTERS

Buried beneath the sands of time
In the deepest waters known to man
Ancient civilizations and pyramids stand
Searching for historic clues is the plan

Buildings exhumed from the ground
Old ships found at the bottom of the sea
Many of the relics brought to the surface
Put into museums and broadcasted on TV

Archeologists dig for the answers
Putting together the puzzle of the past
Trying to uncover every little hint
Not finding every one, still looking for the last

Some of the pieces are found by mistake
For others, they know just where to look
Working on a project until it is completed
So it can be recorded in history's book

The history hunters' job is long and hard work
Always searching the 4 corners of the lands
To seek out history's tales where ever they lurk
Uncovering the past from history's hands.

HISTORY'S MYSTERIES

The pyramids of Egypt are built in the sand
The faces of Mt. Rushmore carved from the rock
The Sphynx is the figure of a cat that is grand
In the city of Baltimore, the ship, Constellation sits in the dock

The ruins of civilizations have many stories to tell
The remains of Machupichu, perched up high
Historians study how these societies fell
For time and seasons people looked toward the sky

The mystery of Stonehenge baffles science to this day
Why do the giant stones stand erect?
How and why was it built? Nobody can say
Archeologists study how these structures were wrecked

History holds many secrets, buried in the sands of time
A lot of questions we will never find answers for
Engineering marvels of geniuses in their prime
Searching for clues to find what history has in store.

PROGRESSION OF MAN

In the beginning there was no technology
The earth was forming through geology
Tools were simple to the prehistoric man
To construct things easier, he had a plan

A hammer and chisel were some of the first made
After the wheel soon came the blade
Putting an edge on stone, now it would cut
Building a home with no door that would shut

The first dwellings were made from rock
Inventing new things gave man a shock
Making new things from wood, clay, & straw
Always improving, he gave it his all

As time progressed, so did his brain
Getting smarter with new knowledge to gain
Structures got bigger; he also made a car
Taking to the air, he built a plane to fly far

Technology growing, there is every new machine
Making life easier and keeping things clean
What next? There's a new invention every day
Since the prehistoric era, man has come a long way.

CASTLE WALLS

Taken back in the time of a castle
After 12 years of school, you get your tassel
In the 1500's, a few hundred years ago
The years flying by, they're no longer slow

The castle walls are built brick by brick
Growing ivy and slime make them slick
Hard to gain access, built on a big hill
Making it to the gates can be a big thrill

Getting to the front door & never getting in
The protective servants fight beside their kin
The main objective is to protect at all cost
If the enemy gains entry, all will be lost

At the top of the towers the flag flies proud
Inside is the king and peasants in the crowd
Safe inside the walls, in the courtyard everyone is together
With no roof overhead, they see all types of weather

Holes in the walls protect those inside
The confines of the stones are very wide
The walls can be 3 ft. thick or more
The old times showing by the clothes they wore

The job is of the bowmen and every able knight
With the advancing army there will be a fight
In the European nation are castles of the middle ages
Lifetimes are written down in history's pages.

HOLOCAUST

In the mid 1940's, the dictator was bold
Soldiers under his command did what they were told
Jews were slaughtered by the day and by the thousand
In camps like Dachau, Auschwitz, and Sachsenhausen

The Chancellor of Germany seduced many with a lying tongue
Anyone who crossed him would be shot, gassed, or hung
Adolf Hitler committed crimes against humanity in his day
The dead buried in the trenches where they lay

Hitler's plan was to exterminate a race
Making ashes in the ovens trying to hide every trace
Into the gas chambers, prisoners were led like sheep
Never coming out, they were induced into eternal sleep

The concentration camps were the tool that he used
In the murder factories, thousands were tortured & abused
The victims were brought to the death camps by train
Some knew what was coming; in their head there was pain

Heinrick Himmler & Hans Stark, 2 of Hitler's closest men
Giving the orders for mass murder, the dead piled in a pen
Scores of bodies in the ovens were turned to ash
Dumped into piles, taken out like bags of trash

It's hard to understand, how these troops could do such a thing
Never questioning their morals with the death that they bring
They didn't feel sorry and there were no signs of remorse
With the world finding out, stopping Hitler would take force

In the Nazi death camps there were few that would survive
Tracking down The Furher, they would never get him alive
The Nazi SS troops had no compassion or grace
If Nazi Germany never came to be, the world would have
been a better place.

AUSCHWITZ-BIRKENAU

After 60 years have gone by
In Poland is where the place is located
On a burial ground where many Jews lie
Because by the Nazi Party they were hated

Hundreds of thousands of humans were decimated
Extermination was the ultimate plan
Lifeless bodies were buried or cremated
How could one human do this to his fellow man?

Trying to create the 'Master Race'
The sign at the gate says "Work Makes You Free"
The dead pile up at an alarming pace
If not shot, they were gassed with Zyklon B

Gassing rooms that resembled a shower
Inhaling the disinfecting agent until they collapsed
The genocide continuing hour after hour
The total number of deceased rose as time elapsed

A quiet cemetery remains where many once stood
Where many were murdered with no regret
How this could take place may be never understood
A part of history the world will never forget.

THE OLD WEST

Riding through town on a horse drawn carriage
Located on the corner is the local saloon
The horses are tied up on a pole outside
As a cowboy on the porch is whistling a tune

These were the times of the wild, wild, west
Where the tumbleweeds rolled and the roads were dirt
Everyone around town carried a gun
Seems in those days it was easy to get hurt

Cowboys like Billy The Kid & The Lone Ranger
Were famous people, which rode the plains
There were the notorious ones always in trouble
For cattle rustling and robbing the trains

With the cowboys and the Indians gone
Is now a ghost town with no population
Old wood buildings and dust blowing around
People headed west with the gold fascination

The wagon trains traveled throughout the Midwest
Ambushed by the Indians and the gunslingers
The roots of country music came from this time
With people making a living as country & western singers

Traveling by horse, wagon, train or foot
In those days was the only way to get around
The small towns today are now deserted
The ruins of which in the south & west can be found.

CHAPTER V – RELIGION / FAITH

MISSION OF THE MESSIAH

In biblical times, buildings were made of mud and stone
The King of Kings is seated at the right side of the throne
Born of the flesh and persecuted by man
To save the world from sin is His master plan

Setting the example and rejecting not a soul
Helping those who ask and fulfilling His earthly role
Accused of blasphemy when only speaking the truth
Teaching the Rabbis and Elders while only in His youth

Making the blind see, and also raising the dead
The Lord fed 5000 with 2 fish and 5 pieces of bread
Jesus knowing His fate, by one of His own He was betrayed
In the Garden of Gethsemane, to The Father, Christ prayed

Satan has no power in Heaven; The Lord is the boss
Christ's mission was fulfilled with Him hanging on the cross
Even facing death, He saved the criminal by His side
Asking Jesus for forgiveness, Paradise was not denied

Living a perfect life in the Middle Eastern land
Even death could not bind Jesus, being raised by God's hand
For God so loved the world, he sent his only Son
Father, Son, and Holy Spirit; The Trinity, which is 3 in 1.

THE ALMIGHTY

The Lord giveth and the Lord taketh away
Life comes through the womb with a black heart
Living is not guaranteed from day to day
It's an up-hill battle from the very start

Living a righteous life can be challenging at times
All praise to the Trinity on high
Forgiveness of all wrong-doings and crimes
God is the key to Heaven's Gate in the sky

About 2000 years ago in a city in the Middle East
A child was born by a virgin in the stable
Later in his life, in the Upper Room there was a feast
With unleavened bread and wine on the table

Jesus was the name of this little child
By his hand many are healed
Kicked out of Heaven, Satan runs wild
Through prophets and the word, the future is revealed

He was sent to save the world
Crucified on a cross with thorns on His head
From the non-believers, insults were hurled
His mission was completed by the blood He shed

3 days after death He lay in the grave
When people returned He was not there
God over-ruling death, took Jesus from the cave
The message of His life would spread everywhere.

FAITH

On the television they say they have found Noah's Ark
But the doubters are never sure of the facts that are real
There are some that read into the truth too much
It's all right in front of them, there is nothing to reveal.

There are some that often speculate
They say it may not be the actual thing
The book of Geneses tells them where it's located
If they read the 'Good Book', maybe they would learn something

There is an article in Italy known as 'The Shroud'
Scientists are trying to figure out who the image may be
They run many tests & come up with no real answer
All the signs are on the cloth…Who is in the image? You tell me.

Keep an eye on the news, and look at the signs of the times
The world is getting close to the end days
There are wars, rumors of wars, and a lot of turmoil
In the very end the road of life will split, the only choice is 1
of 2 ways.

I hope you choose wisely to get where you want to go
There will be some that will not make the grade
Their pain & suffering will get worse as time goes on
The signs in your life will tell you if the right choice was made.

THE HOLIDAY SEASON

The holiday season is around the corner
Busy shopping days will soon be here
With fall approaching, days are getting shorter
For businesses, higher sales will appear

The day after Thanksgiving, consumers hit the mall
Buying things for Christmas Day
Reading the sale ads and hearing their call
Paying the bills beyond the month of May

December is the most joyous time of the year
Celebration of the Christ child being born
At the end of November the days draw near
The 25th of December, wrapping paper will be torn

November and December are the months of shopping
The real meaning of Christmas we must keep in mind
People spending past their limit without stopping
Society's way of thinking needs to be refined

Once the numbers are tallied
Then the cards can be scored
Around the dollar, the business is rallied
People spend hard earned money that many can't afford

At the holiday time, let us never lose our sight
In the word Christmas, Christ is the main reason
Wake up from the dark and look into the light
Jesus entering this world is the meaning of the holiday season.

THE HOLY ONE

He is the King of all Kings
The Glorious One on high
Born into this world as a child
Leaving this place, ascending to the sky

Healing the sick and afflicted
His place is to the right of the throne
Setting the perfect example for which to live
In biblical times, He became well known

Performing miracles on the most wicked
By a multitude His name was smeared
His purpose here was to fulfill prophecy
By His hand, clouded vision is cleared

Gaining followers as years progressed
Leading them until His death on the cross
Once resurrected and leaving planet earth
Some considered His life to be a loss

Giving up His flesh body on earth
Returning to Heaven with The Father by His side
The Holy Spirit still exists in the world
To receive salvation, in The Lord you must confide!

DIVINE INFLUENCE

Society teaches the concept of evolution
Lying to children about how we came to be
For any problem of this world, God is the solution
Sending his son Jesus Christ to die for you & me

In the first few books of The Bible
Are where the basic laws of life were made
Since then, man has added his own rules
The 1st ten laws written in stone will never fade

Prophecies were made in the books of the old
Telling & warning people of future events
As people rebelled; men's hearts grew hard & cold
A person can obtain Salvation if he or she repents

The Ultimate Sacrifice was born in a small town
A child in a stable, Jesus Christ being His name
The King of the Jews wore thorns as a crown
To save the world from sin is the reason He came

Many miracles He performed in His day
Healing the sick & blind and raising Lazarus from death
The religious rulers didn't know what to say
Life in the womb is created by God's breath

The people made fun of and mocked The Lord
Letting the murderer Barabbas go free
'Crucify Him, Crucify Him' is what the crowd roared
His earthly life ended with Him hanging on a tree

Accept Jesus in your heart while there is still time
With tomorrow never promised, there may not be another day
Rid yourself of all sin, wrong-doing, and crime
And see for yourself, Jesus is the Truth, the Life, & the Way.

DEFEAT OF EVIL WAYS

From the foundation of the world
The first verse of Genesis says "In the beginning…"
God made everything with perfection
The works of Satan started mankind sinning

From that day in the Garden of Eden
Mankind enters the world born into sin
Accept now the gift of salvation
Defeating Satan, in the end, God will win!

With Jesus accepted into the heart
The Holy Spirit can now produce fruit
Walking in the ways of the Lord
Will strengthen the spiritual root

God created a creature called man
Formed from the earth's dirt and dust
Traveling down the road of life
For happiness and peace, in God we must trust

God reconciling Himself to us
Humanly born and lived as a man
Coming to save the world and not condemn it
Performing miracles and works like only God can

Man has followed the ways of the world
Some men now take a husband instead of a wife
Immorality and perversion fill the earth
The only way to Heaven is having Jesus in your life

God wishes for not 1 soul to perish
His desire is for all to be saved
Many need to change their way of living
Or suffer the punishment for the way that they behaved

Religion and politics are hot issues
People trying to take God out of everything
Separation from God will result in destruction
The day of His wrath, evildoers will feel His sting

After Jesus ascended back into Heaven
The promise of the Holy Spirit was sent
Turn from your sins and turn to the Lord
He will come again in the same manner He went.

THE GOOD BOOK

The history of the world is contained in these pages
Different things occurring throughout the ages
Things coming together in various stages
A battle between good and evil wages

Powerful words are in this authoritative book
Important contents with nothing to overlook
A manual on how to live a prosperous life
In times of joy and through times of strife

Written by people who were divinely inspired
To be chosen from above was all that was required
Through the prophets, the stories were told
Of future events, that in time, would unfold

Since its printing, it is the all-time best seller
Not one book can compare; its message is stellar
The good news inside is second to none
Applied to human lives, souls will be won

Divided into two parts, the Old and the New
Not one false statement, every word is true
Fake religions and their ideas are its biggest rival
For truth and ways to overcome evil,
Look into the contents of The Holy Bible!

THANK YOU

Thank you Lord for Your wonderful works
For easing man's pain, inside where it hurts
Thank you for Your comfort and Your love
Surrounding our mind & soul like a tight fitting glove

Thank you Father for the great things You have done
May Your name be magnified with each soul that is won
Thank you God for giving us Your written word
Instructing us how to act, when things seem so absurd

Thank you O God, for sending Your only Son
That we may reside with You when all is said and done
May Your name be glorified and praised every day
Thank you Jesus for hearing us when we pray

Thank you Lord for each blessing You bestow
Speak to our hearts, that we may spiritually grow
Thank you Holy One for Your mercy and Your grace
At the end of time, may we meet You face to face

Thank you Almighty for Your gift of salvation
Through Your Son we are saved from eternal damnation
Thank you Heavenly Father for just being who you are
In good times and bad, You are our shining star

I would like to thank you from the bottom of my heart
For saving my soul from sin, for giving me a fresh start
In everything I do, may Your name be praised
When we all get to Heaven, we will all be amazed!

BEING RIGHT WITH GOD

With the power of Christ in you
Things thought impossible can be done
Within the corrupted and evil world
There are none that are perfect, no, not one

Once accepting Jesus as savior
In dark times and conflict, you are never alone
Keeping the Lord first priority in your life
Now is the time for the seeds to be sewn

The ways of man are insignificant to God
We can do nothing of our own ability
In the presence of the Lord & in time of prayer
Approach him with humbleness and humility

Since the time of Adam and Eve
People enter life in the bondage of sin
There is joy and victory through Jesus Christ
And the gift of the Holy Spirit that dwells within

The day of the Lord is drawing near
We are now living in the end times
Unbelievers must stand before the throne
To be judged for their wickedness and their crimes

Resist the devil and keep your heart pure
With the gift of salvation we are saved from sin
Together with the Lord, we will all be in Heaven
When this takes place, your new life will begin.

WONDROUS WORKS

Listening to the speaker's testimony
Through his words, God moves the heart
The message sows seeds for the Lord
After being watered, germination will start

Usually with different people involved
No one person completes the task
The Spirit moves in the midst of the crowd
To receive Jesus, all you need to do is ask

Praising the Lord for His wondrous works
Calling on the Lord, He will answer prayer
Not when we expect it but in His perfect timing
God will never leave you, for He is everywhere

When everything seems to be going OK
And even in times of trouble and strife
Mankind can do nothing on his own
Turn your eyes upon Jesus and give Him your life

God will grant you everything you need
Every blessing received comes from above
Give God all the praise, glory, and honor
For gifts freely given and His unconditional love.

END OF LIFE

From the very first moment of birth
Begins the journey of life until your dying day
Cherish the time you have here on earth
In the twinkling of an eye it can be taken away

Every living thing must taste death
Every person will be placed in the grave
Live life for the Lord with each breath
With faith and belief in Jesus, your soul He will save

Many people fear the day they will die
Because they do not know what to expect
The loss of someone close will cause them to cry
Within each person there is a similar effect

One product of death is a feeling of despair
People are more sensitive with each word said
The world is not perfect, nor is life fair
Jesus paid our ransom with the blood that He shed

The ending of life is never a fun thing
Jesus sent the Comforter to help us with the pain
He takes away the sorrow and feeling of death's sting
With God in your life, you have everything to gain

Jesus conquered death by resurrection from the grave
Going back to the Father, He will one day come again
God sent His son into a world He desired to save
Who knows the day or hour? Only the Father knows when.

JESUS SAVES

Each need is known, for God reads the heart
When Christ is accepted as Savior, the soul is set apart
The Holy Spirit is then sent to you from above
The gift of salvation is a confirmation of God's love

The evilness of the prior life is now put away
The Spirit dwells within you, in your heart He will stay
A changed life shows the power of the Lord
It is the only gift that anyone can afford

Trust in Jesus and put your life into His hand
In times of temptation and trouble, He will help you stand
With life in Christ, you can draw power from His name
All good deeds and efforts will be tested by His flame

Store your treasure in Heaven, not in worldly greed
Jesus paid the debt so slaves of sin could be freed
The Roman custom of crucifixion was the way He died
The result of His death, to man a lifeline was supplied

His resurrection made it possible for God to save mankind
Just call on His name and you won't be left behind
The method in which Jesus left, He will return the same way
God's children look forward to their redemption day

Taken out of a sinful world, with the Lord they will be
On that awesome day, the face of their Savior they will see
You can be there also, believe on God's only begotten Son
The battle of good vs. evil, by the Lord will finally be won.

DON'T FORGET TO PRAY

There are many people in the world today
Who claim to be Christians but forget to pray
It's amazing to know we can go to the Lord in prayer
His name can be called upon anytime and anywhere

The Father reads the heart; He knows what you want to say
Jesus paid the debt that we could never repay
Prayers are taken to God, by Jesus the Holy Son
Trust in the Lord brings victory when all is said and done

Look into His word, where there is so much to learn
Dying without Jesus will cause your soul to burn
Give your heart to the Lord, along with every care
The Holy Spirit will guide you when life seems so unfair

When Jesus left this world, He promised He would return
God already knows your every burden and concern
Pray never ceasing to your Heavenly Father above
With the ability to look past our sin, that's the power of God's
love.

GOD'S GIFT OF SALVATION

Are you saved or are you not sure?
Lift your head and look on high
In any problem or condition, the Lord is the cure
God's love for us is the reason Jesus was sent to die

For God so loved the world, He sent His only Son
The ultimate sacrifice, paying the debt for our sin
The enemy's work is not yet done
There is victory in Jesus for the war raging within

There is only one sure way to enter Heaven's gate
Accept Jesus in your heart while you still have time
Our days here are numbered, tomorrow may be too late
His forgiveness covers any offense or crime

Being nailed to the cross, He died for you and me
His blood was shed so that we may live
Share your faith in Jesus with others that you see
The Lord is waiting and wanting to forgive.

BEFORE THE CRUCIFIXION

Celebrating the Lord's Supper
Partaking of the cup and the bread
Signifying the body of Christ
And His precious blood that was shed

Speaking to His disciples in the upper room
Jesus said, "Do this in remembrance of Me"
To keep Him in the forefront of our minds
To have faith in that which we cannot see

Going to the place called Gethsemane
It was here where Jesus prayed
Asking for the pain and suffering to pass
By a man named Judas, Christ was betrayed

Before the foundation of the world
The perfect sacrifice for sin was needed
Beaten, ridiculed, mocked, and crucified
Rising from the grave, death was defeated

Ascending back to the Father's right hand
His mission on earth was now complete
When the Day of the Lord comes to pass
We will all stand before His judgment seat

Some will receive eternal punishment
For believers there will be a reward to receive
Then there will be that awesome day
When eternal life is given to those who believe.

OPPOSITION IN HEAVEN

The Lord is my shield and my protection
Jesus came by Immaculate Conception
Sinners are saved by the Lord's redemption
Made possible by His death & resurrection

The joy of Jesus is with His believers
Christians are attacked by evil deceivers
Pain and sorrow are upon all grievers
Preaching the gospel, the hearers are receivers

When Jesus was here, He walked many places
When He taught, He spoke to many faces
Being everywhere, He occupies many spaces
Was He accepted where he went? Not in many cases

He's always with us everywhere we go
We read & study His word and spiritually we grow
The destiny of unbelievers is only filled with woe
Contending with the adversary, Satan is His foe

Jesus enters the heart; the change comes from within
Those who enter Heaven on their faces will be a grin
Since Satan's expulsion, God has been fighting sin
In the 'Great Day of the Lord', God will eternally win!

THE LORD'S GLORY

We cannot begin to comprehend
The awesomeness of the Lord's glory
Nobody has ever seen God's face and lived
Throughout The Bible, which is His story

The face of Moses glowed so bright
In front of other people he had to wear a veil
The glory reflected was unbearable to see
With the Lord in his life, Moses couldn't fail

Moses caught a glimpse after the Lord passed by
That must have been a sight to behold
When believers receive their glorified bodies
We will have something that is finer than gold

Imagine what Moses must have thought
The Lord's miracles performed by his hand
The 10 plagues and the parting of the sea
Our limited minds can't begin to understand

These were other things that Moses saw
A burning bush & his stick become a snake
To the right hand of God, Jesus was exalted
The only Man in history to never make a mistake

Once all Christians are granted access into Heaven
We will meet our Maker and Moses will be there
The glory of Heaven and seeing our Lord
Awestruck by Jesus, in His glory we will share

When that day comes, will you be there?
Turn your life over to Jesus while you are able
Don't miss out on the festivities of Heaven
There is room for all at the Lord's table.

A QUICK JOURNEY
THROUGH THE WORD

Since the beginning of time was the Divine Creator
By His hand the foundation of the earth was laid
His handiwork includes all that we see
For His glory and purposes everything was made

God created man in His own image
The Garden of Eden was man's place to dwell
Sin entered the world by Satan's temptation
Seducing as many as he can by his evil spell

Early in history God revealed Himself to man
To people like Noah, Moses, and David the king
The Lord gave us His word through His prophets
God's instructions for life is the message they bring

After the time of the prophets of old
Was a period of silence for 400 years
Throughout the Old Testament were many battles
The tools used were swords, shields, and spears

Soon after John the Baptist was born
A virgin named Mary was about to give birth
The news spread fast in the town of Bethlehem
That the Savior of the world was arriving on earth

The ministry of Jesus spread through the land
There were many corrupted souls to win
God gave us His Son to die on the cross
By His death and resurrection, He conquered death & sin

After Jesus ascended back to the Father
The apostles were to preach the good news
Many people received the gift of salvation
Accepting Jesus, there's no way you can lose

The apostle Paul wrote many letters
To help the new churches along their way
Instructing them by divine revelations
On how to live their lives day by day

Prophecy is written at the very end
Of signs of the times & events that will soon be
Then Jesus will return and rule the world
This will culminate the world's history

Accept Jesus as your Lord and Savior
This could be the day, before it's too late
Turn your eyes upon Jesus and live for the Lord
For the assurance of admission into Heaven's gate.

TRUST IN HIM

The Lord will fight your battles for you
Step out on faith and trust in Him
Keep your eyes focused and do not worry
He will answer the question of whether you sink or swim

Look at the story of Moses in days of old
The power of the Lord brought them through the sea
He delivered Israel from their adversary
He can do similar things for you or for me

To activate God's power there must be faith
Without it, you can't expect to be blessed
For the person with Jesus in their heart
He relieves the feeling of being down and distressed

God sometimes works in mysterious ways
The works of His hands are not always seen
There are times you must look below the surface
To get a full grasp on what things really mean

People often take many things personally
Asking the question, 'Why did this happen to me?'
Sometimes they are used for the purpose of another
The reasons are not always obvious to see

There will be a day when all questions are answered
Exercise your faith & hope so it will stay strong
Keep studying in the truths of God's Word
Applying the Word to your life, you can't go wrong

Trust in the Lord with all your heart
In His judgments He is just and fair
God's believing people need not be troubled
It's the rejecters of God that need to beware!

MY AFTERLIFE

When I finally get to Heaven
Jesus will be the first that I seek
Looking forward to this moment all my life
Face to face with my Savior I will speak

Or will I stand in amazement,
Feeling petrified with fear?
Being awestruck, speechless, and silent
As I see the Holy One draw near

After the issues of life have passed
The afterlife is soon to begin
Wanting to personally thank Jesus
For setting me free from the bondage of sin

Will there be the 'light at the end of the tunnel'?
Many mysteries are to be revealed
Our limited minds cannot comprehend
My future with my Savior is forever sealed

Not knowing exactly what to expect
Leaving this body I will immediately see
Pain and suffering being a thing of the past
In the presence of the Lord I will eternally be!

THE LOVE OF THE LORD

It's quiet outside, like the earth stood still
Everything happens according to God's will
The reduction of noise is a sign of His peace
As soon as man awakes confusion will increase

His Spirit in our hearts rids us of the strife
Belief in the Son of God will bring eternal life
Willingly leaving Heaven, He came to hang on a tree
Giving up His life, He shed His blood for you and me

His life was an example for everyone to see
His human life ended on the Hill of Calvary
A man without sin, He is perfect in every way
Being putty in His hands, He molds us like we are clay

His love for us is true; He provides our every need
Telling others of His love, we plant a holy seed
As we rely on the Lord, His people He will bless
Forgiveness of our sins requires us to confess

Many treasures are found in His Holy Book we read
He knows our every move, thought, word, and deed
Is there sickness, He is the cure, the one and only source
Can He make a difference in your life? The answer is of
course!

CHAPTER VI –
INDUSTRY & OBJECTS

F-117 STEALTH

Deep in the Nevada and New Mexico desert
A place so remote, the pilots are flown in
Secrets being kept while tests are being done
Of an odd shaped plane with a black tail fin

Operators stay for a week at a time
To make sure the bird is ready for flight
It has no curves but many different angles
Its primary mission is conducted at night

Being a technological breakthrough
A radar evading fighter jet
Look and listen & never see it coming
The ordinance impacts where the laser is set

Costing between 46 and 52 million dollars
Showing in the Iraq war it's worth the price
All the missions flown and not 1 loss
It's a dangerous and deadly war device

New projects on the horizon
Stealth technology rules the air
A new tool for the U.S. Air Force
To put to use in times of warfare

Some call it a flying ghost
Flying undetected and never seen
This plane is referred to as the Nighthawk
Also know as the Stealth F-117.

THE ASPHALT JUNGLE

Highways get you from 1 place to another
Asphalt laid where vehicles can drive
Some have 3 lanes or more in which to travel
With many accidents yearly, some won't survive

There are those who try to drive fast
They must think they're in a race
The cars on the right; always being passed
It seems they can't keep up with the pace

Miles of roadway stretch from state to state
With painted lines of yellow and white
Backed up traffic that accidents create
Everyone slows down so they can see the sight

Many signs posted tell you which direction to travel
The interstates have rest areas where many cars stop
In the country the roads are made of dirt or gravel
On either side you may see the farmers crop

In Germany it's called the Autobahn
A strip where speed demons can go fast
It's a highway many Americans have never driven on
A different way of driving is quite a contrast

Where does it start, where does it end?
The asphalt jungle goes from coast to coast
Crossing 1 border to another the road will extend
Into the next state or country the highway will host

There is a phenomenon called 'Road Rage'
At any little thing the drivers get irate
Trying to compete on a blacktop stage
Watch out for these drivers; welcome to the interstate.

THE INFORMATION AGE

In the old days there was only radio
Then came television and the press
Before the year 2000 the Internet was introduced
The computer industry became a success

People get the news from every available source
The most popular being newspapers or T.V.
Now it is gained by a keyboard and a monitor
Microsoft, Dell, and Apple market the P.C.

The competition is between Michael Dell & Bill Gates
Who is ahead in the technology game?
These two are at the top of computer sales
Who has more money? Right now Gates is the name

Reporters in the field go after the top stories
They ascertain the facts and information
They are available any time, night or day
It seems every day there is a new situation

In magazines and on billboards ads are found
About a product a company wants to sell
Signs are posted along every road
Do people actually read them? The sales figures will tell

Some information travels by word-of-mouth
People sharing experiences they have had
Consumers will return to a business they trust
Petty merchants with no customers are the ones that are mad

You will hear about news from all over the world
Stories and facts are gathered from every source
Reporters travel many hours and many miles
They are the press and the media's workhorse

Now with computers in millions of homes
The news reaches the masses very fast
Instead of waiting from one Sunday to the next
From 1 source to another, information is passed.

INDUSTRY

Paper is something made in the mill
A product of wood pulp, which comes from trees
The logs are hauled down from the hill
There are different lengths and sizes of these

Once cut down the trucks take them away
Each year the Forrest is getting thin
On an office desk you will find paper in a tray
On a shelf in a bar, a bottle of gin

Raw materials are dug out of the earth
Some of the products are gems, steel, and rocks
Also the diamonds, which carry much worth
The jewelry market has a rise in stocks

The ore is extracted by blasting a hole
The workers go into the mine
The boundary of the workplace is marked by a pole
The jobless stand in the unemployment line

Customers are the key in the company's sales
Without them no money will be made
Products are transported by trucks, boats, or rails
In New York on Wall Street, the stock market is played

Gasoline prices rise but demand is the same
Production was cut back for barrels of crude
Oil companies need refineries to stay in the game
The oil rich countries are giving people a bad attitude

Farmers are planting seeds in the soil
Their machines are working to harvest their crops
Many of the plants are safe to eat if they boil
Without the rain their total drops

Products are traded based on the country's need
Things they can't produce they wish to acquire
Working for years for a property deed
After 25 or 30 years of service, you're ready to retire.

U.S. NAVY BLUE ANGELS

Arriving one day before the show
Watching the practice of high speed jets
Planes that travel past the speed of sound
Pilots with parachutes but no safety nets

The color of the aircraft vary
Being camouflage or battleship gray
A demonstration of the 'Blue Angels' perform
On the first chilly overcast day

The team is flying the F-18 Hornet
A fighter, top speed close to mach 2
Performing stunts that awe the crowd
Keeping them flying is the Blue Angel crew

The tails are numbered 1..2..3..
There are 7 planes in all
A show requiring the utmost attention
A drill team flying with little or no flaw

At times in the air they're only 3 ft. apart
There is no room for any mistake
Their signature formation being the 'Blue Diamond'
Performing maneuvers that really 'take the cake'

Once the performance is completed
The pilots are safely back on the ground
Headed for the next exciting show
On another military base they will be found.

WORKING A LIFETIME

Up early every morning around the hour of 4
Get some coffee; leave the house, lock the door
Going to work punching the clock, always the same time
Working to pay bills, trying to earn every dime

Performing well you give them your best
At the end of the day your body cries for rest
Work hard and always do a good job
Get fired or laid off and join the unemployed mob

Working for 'The Man', unlikely you'll get rich
No matter if you're a manager or even digging a ditch
Some days are long, could be 12 hrs. or longer
Whatever doesn't kill you only makes you stronger

Hunting for the largest salaries that are paid
Whether it be a doctor, lawyer, or even working a trade
Putting in the years to obtain a decent vacation
Looking forward to retirement, you're in it for the duration

Give them 20 yrs. Then they ask you for 5 or 10 more
Quit while you're ahead, never knowing what the future has
in store
After such a long time its finally retirement day
Time for someone else to take over, now everything is okay.

PACTIV CORPORATION

Plastic pellets fall from the train car to the ground
There are people not working when the bosses aren't around
Trying to save money, cutting corners here and there
Watching the machines, employees sit and stare

Maintenance is called several times a day
One thing every employee does is worry about the pay
The production line never operates as planned
At the end of shift, by the time clock they will stand

Striving for 0 accidents, each month we have a meeting
As people have a seat, donuts they are eating
Meeting attendance is mandatory; workers need to stay
Everyone is tired after working a 12-hour day

Disappearing for the weekend only to return
Later is a fire drill so in an emergency people won't burn
Making products of quality is what customers look for
Many have come and gone through the company's rotating
door

Resin costs go up as the price continues to rise
Which translates into a lot of money for a company of this size
Dozens of the 'old timers' have much vacation time
The up and coming company is now in it's prime.

AIRPLANE

A vehicle that flies high in the air
It's constructed like a tube with wings
For the right amount you can have a 1ˢᵗ class chair
Movies, drinks, snacks, and other things

A fast way to travel, flying high in the sky
The airplane is the way to go
Some people are afraid to fly
Above the clouds there's no rain, no snow

Watching the news, eventually you will see
A story of a crash is sure to be found
The engines are big with lots of energy
The flight is over with the plane back on the ground

Made to get from one place to another
Anti-Americans use it for purposes that are bad
In N.Y. City on September 11, America thought ' OH
BROTHER!'
On Sept. 12ᵗʰ 2001, there were many Americans that were
sad.

DIFFERENT MODES OF TRAVEL

A tube made of metal with wings made of steel
The airplane requires 2 operators at the wheel
It cruises at an altitude around 30,000 feet
Some painted with different colors to enhance its appeal

Trains haul cargo and passengers as well
The ones in N.Y. City are decorated with pastel
With horns so loud they can almost wake the dead
To board trains or planes you need tickets that they sell

The tour bus, like a car, rides on the street
Depending on their size, different capacities they can seat
The trip is slower than an airplane or a train
Some destinations are so close; the fastest way is your feet

Boats float on the water from sea to shining sea
When the Titanic sank in the ocean the people tried to flee
The weather can hinder the voyage from 1 port to another
All of these means of travel are expensive; nobody rides for
free.

18 WHEELERS

Trucks are used to carry supplies into battle
Bringing merchandise to any type of store
From the farms they're used to haul cattle
A transport for troops in time of war

Most big rigs have 18 wheels
With a fifth wheel on the back of the cab
On the doors of the trailer some have seals
Trucks in the military painted in olive drab

The most common trailers are flatbed or box
Used to carry all sorts of things
Open top dumpers are used to haul rocks
Cargo held on the trailers by belts and slings

The tractor's take off is very slow
The large vehicles have many gears
A lot of trucks are lined in a row
What is known as a convoy now appears

Holding up traffic on highway roads
Big rigs not being the fastest thing around
Being slower when they pull the heavy loads
Not stopping quickly, it takes a while to slow down

Hauling things where ever there is a need
Getting goods and products to a destination
Built for power and not for speed
Traveling coast to coast and all over the nation.

THE WAREHOUSE

A building with much square footage
With usually more than one dock door
Products packed up to the ceiling
In a rack or stacked in rows on the floor

Trailers arrive at the company all day long
Filled with products unloaded at the dock
When the trailer is empty and the doors are closed
The warehouse workers will soon be off the clock

The structure has very high ceilings
Sometimes being 20 feet or higher
A storage place for lots of goods
An evacuation route in needed in case of fire

Some days the building is close to empty
On other days its almost over filled
Safety is a key issue for the workers
The floor must be clean with nothing spilled

Merchandise is always coming or going
Within the walls it's a busy place
The flow of goods never stops moving
Items appearing and disappearing case by case

A necessary part of the business
A place where finished product is stocked
The warehouse is found in every city
On weekends & holidays the door will be locked.

MAINTENANCE MAN

Going to work strapped with a leather pouch
Hitting the thumb with a hammer, you can hear him yell
OUCH!
The purpose for the pouch is to hold lots of tools
Having a hard day on the job, working like mules

Armed with a toolbox, a ladder, and a truck
Repairing broken machines when people are having bad luck
Sometimes something simple like replacing a tiny fuse
Working around the shop he must wear safety shoes

On an easy day everything is running good
Then there are days when things don't run as they should
Needing a boost, he goes to get the ladder
To fix the problem he has to find out what's the matter

Having the hardware like nuts, bolts, and screws
For large businesses there are groups of maintenance crews
Being the handyman, it seems there's nothing they can't fix
Turning the electricity on, it's the switch that he flicks

Everything is now operating well
There are no further issues as far as he can tell
A long hard day feeling exhausted and beat
Everything running properly, his job is complete.

CHAPTER VII –
FRIENDS & PEOPLE

Note:
All feelings are not the same now as they were then. Some of
the poems in this chapter are from past relationships before I
was happily married in March 2001.

CO-WORKER

Listening to the man at work
He likes the older music with much guitar
He's a very quiet, soft-spoken soul
Sometimes he speaks like he wants to be a star

Sometimes of lots of money
Many times of the T-Bone steaks
I try to explain to him how to get there
I'm not hurtin' but that's the breaks

I've got my share of bills
In no sense am I rich
Just think about what you do,
I had to dig out of a 7 year ditch

Nothing was ever given to me
I've earned everything I have ever had
Just stop, think, & make wise decisions
And maybe one day you will have your own pad

Maybe one day he will figure it out
And decide what's best for his life
Getting a partner in life isn't a bad thing,
Your best friend could end up being your wife.

TRAFFIC ACCIDENT (9-25-04)

When the road is wet, people still drive too fast
If involved in an accident, your 1st could be your last
Following too close was the reason for today
A 24 car pile-up occurred on the I-35 highway

In the opposite direction on the other side of the road
In north and southbound lanes, traffic was slowed
2 separate crashes, each with 6 cars
In all, no fatalities, people only had cuts & scars

It all started with a car hydroplaning in the street
There were many crashed vehicles on the concrete
50 people were treated; all went home alive
When behind the wheel there's no promise you will arrive

In most cases, operator error is the reason
Crashes happen day or night and in every season
Careless drivers should go back to school
To learn to operate a car as a safe and useful tool

When in bad weather, drivers need to drive with care
With others on the road, to them it's only fair
Any type of accident can easily take a life
The next one could involve your children or your wife

Driving today is a matter of life and death
It could be you at any time, taking your last breath
Many crashes that happen, people can prevent
Don't be a statistic in the next vehicular accident.

TAKING OF A LIFE

What kind of person is this?
Committing murder in the 1st degree
What makes him think he can take a life?
Leaving the victims' loved ones in misery

The nation's correctional facilities are full of them
Inmates serving a sentence for the killing
Depriving another human being of their years
The weapon of gun or knife, the blood ends up spilling

Working in a jail, seeing them come and go
Some leaving a better person than they came
The lifetime criminals' heads will never change
For those with life & no parole, every day is the same

Murder is against the 10 Commandments
For it states "Thou shall not kill"
People with strange and corrupted minds
For their crimes they must pay the bill

If everyone could just get along
This world would be a much better place
There are those on this earth who don't care
Looking at death and spitting in its face

In the end there will finally be eternal peace
After the world has been through its last days
Evil and corruption will be put to rest
The life of the earth as we know it will be in its last phase.

FOR JACKIE

To a good friend; I hate to see you go
I'll miss you much; I think you know
You're out of trouble, I give you praise
I hope I will see you for a few more days

Jacqueline or Jennifer or whatever name you like best
I'll visit you anytime; I would love to be your guest
When I look into your eyes I see innocence like in the eyes of
a child
If I had your telephone number it would definitely be dialed

I came over to see you and you welcomed me in
Most people act different and that made my head spin
Love is a power that makes people act strange
Now I'm getting older my goals I must rearrange

Do I want to party or settle down?
Maybe find a woman and move to another town
If I could find one like you I would be very amused
Then I wouldn't have to worry about my heart being bruised

Inside I'm full of love; I want to give it away
I want to find a nice person like you; maybe another day?
A good person is hard to find; If you get one hold on tight
Be careful with what you have or your dreams won't be in sight

Jackie, Jackie, when you go I wish you the best of luck
Have fun in your future but be careful not to get stuck
I hope you have a good time; take it easy and have a nice ride
Maybe I'll be lucky one day and I'll see you on the other side

VAYA CON DIOS CARINO!

JESSI

March '98

A girl from the club
Gina is her name
She seems different than all others
I hope she's not the same

When I'm free I want to be with her
She makes me feel at ease
She's a wonderful young lady
She acts not like a sleaze

She's got a pretty face
And a fabulous smile
When I see her my feelings soar
For much more than a mile.

Sometimes I feel I'm being played
Because of experiences in the past
Sometimes I don't care what happens
And I try to have a blast.

I feel comfortable when I'm with her
I wish the time would never end
She's an inspiration to my life
My thoughts refuse to bend.

If I ever thought about a wife
Right now she would be my choice
When I look at her picture
In my mind I hear her voice.

She knows how to treat me
She knows what I like best
I feel like I'm in heaven
While she's laying on my chest.

I enjoy the moments I'm with her
Each and every one
I hope there are many more good times
So we can have more fun.

JESSICA, JESSICA

4-98

Jessica, Jessica you are my shining star
When I'm with you my heart has no scar
I want to be with you as much as I can
I want to be everything to you; I want to be your man

When we're together I feel safe like when on dry land
When we're apart my eyes feel like sand
My love for you I don't know how to explain
I can't clear my heart of your love, it falls like rain

When needed I want to be there for you
If we're not meant for each other I need to find someone new
I don't like to think that way, it brings a tear to my eye
Sometimes I want to break down and cry

Jessica, Jessica the name is music to my ear
When I think of you I wish you were near
A sweetheart like you; you are my obsession
Unless treated bad, I have no aggression

Jessica, Jessica I love you
I hope you love me the same way too
Times like this in my life are rare
When I see your face I just want to stare

Te casarias con migo? Is the question of the day
I don't want to ask because I don't know what you will say
I think of the future and it rips my mind in two
What will happen next? I have not a clue.

PANAMA

I'm on my way to Panama
My 2 yrs. in Germany is done
I hope to start speaking the tacos
This elapsed time has been fun.

I arrived at Tocumen Airport
And what did I see?
Juan Valdez and Panama Jack
Staring back at me.

I'm now in another country
Closer to home yet far away
I'm in the middle of the airport thinking
Should I try to speak the spenglish today?

Another gringo in their country
They're probably thinking "Go Home"
I think I'm ready to meet the Senoritas
And make my presence known.

I miss my friends in Germany
But I've met some new ones here
Stay away from the guys near Gorgas
They dress like women and they're queer.

The drivers here are crazy
On the road there is no law
If you dare step out in front of them
The medics you may want to call.

Women in this country are beautiful
Your eyes see every girl
This is one place you will find
Some of the most gorgeous girls in the world.

The girls here are greedy
All they want is what you got
When they take all they can get
They will leave you there to rot.

A good one is hard to find,
A girl that can walk on glass,
Maybe I'll be lucky to find her
And find a babe with class

Life outside of duty is cool
There are many things to see
Take my advice "Don't be a barracks rat"
And waste time watching t.v.

There are lots of places to dive
Go under and see the reef
Be careful when you go downtown
It seems that everyone is a thief.

If you ever come to Panama
Check it out its a cool place
Maybe on the next Journey
I'll take you to outer space.

JODY

Jody, Jody, A name I know well
As I sit here in the desert, this place is hot as hell!
One lonely cloud in the sky, I think of it as me
If I was back at FT. Hood, on the computer is where I would be.

Talking to my friend from another state
With her words that are as smoothe as a marble plate.
When we talk we need to hide from the man,
Now I am blinded by the color of desert tan.

Yesterday was my B-Day, I would have loved to talk to her then
It would have made the day better, Talkin' to my special friend.
From where I sit now, there are mountains on every side.
One of these days the work will pay off, At least I can say I tried.

I miss you now Jody, I'm thinking of you a lot.
What we don't eat, the coyotes will take; nothing is left to rot.
This place looks so dead & desolate to me
The only life I can find is the figure of a ' Joshua Tree'

When the sunset comes the mountain is purple each and every day
I wish I never came to Cali., By your side is where I want to stay.
Each day seems a little hotter; this place is much too warm
I think that I should go now, I think it's goin' to storm!

MY FRIEND

Sitting in the office
It's the radio I hear
I wish I wasn't working
Then my thoughts would be clear

Today started out sunny
Yesterday there was rain
I would like to be traveling with my friend
On a bus, a boat, or a plane

It's been real boring today
There's not much to do
I ponder thoughts of vacation
And wonder, were they true?

It seems that they were real
It was there I met a special friend
I wanted to take this person home
So our cultures we could blend

I don't want to mention this person's name
If they read this poem they will know who they are
Once I leave this place
From my friend I will be far.

I wonder will my friends miss me
When they notice I'm not around
I wonder if they will think of me
Will they ever utter a sound?

I will slowly increase our space
As I move farther and farther away
Then the last day will come
And to my friend I'll have nothing to say.......
Except Goodbye

INSPIRED BY N.D. – 30 SEP. 99

Neriah, Neriah, is music to my ear
I would like to meet her one day,
When I look at her picture I wish she was here
By her side is where I want to stay.

Her body is perfect, curves in the right places
Innocence is the look in her face.
She has long flowing hair like new white laces
I don't know where to find her, she's lost without a trace.

I have many photos of her on my wall
When I look at them my days are better,
I have a new one to put in my hall
This one, with a tight knit sweater.

Her looks are as sharp as a razor; they cut to the bone
If you look too long your eyes will sting.
I would like to call her on the phone
And maybe offer her a ring.

I guess I'll go for now
There is still work to be done,
It will all get done but I don't know how
Probably when there's no more sun!

NAMES

Michele, Michele
It's a name I know well
Sometimes I wish she would come over
Sometimes I say "Oh Well?"

It would be nice for things to work out
But it seems I have the worst luck
Maybe I should keep on traveling
With nothing but my pick-up truck

Now I have met a new chick
One with a name of Dory
Like everything else in life
It's the same old story

I look at the view of the city
Feeling like something is there
But when I go downtown
I wonder why I even care

Maybe it's because of Natalie
Or maybe of her sister,
Sometimes it seems that life
Is spinning like a twister

Daniel, Wendy, or Claudia
It really doesn't matter the name
Because deep inside I know
The outcome is always the same.

INCARCERATED OFFENDER

Behavior is an attitude
Inmates in jail hate the food
For their offense they're sentenced for years
Before the parole board they shed their tears

In the jail yard they get their recreation
Seems they have more rights than people in the free nation
When they don't get their way, they want a grievance report
Anywhere the offender goes; they need an escort

In the jail confines will be found contraband
In every single jail across this land
Having fun to them is messing with the boss
Between inmate and officer is a fine line to cross

A model inmate is the one who acts right
Doing what is required and staying out of the next fight
These offenders get the privileges and the jobs
All the rest are in the gangs and the mobs

Many of the incarcerated act like a child
When time to eat, to the mess hall they are filed
Ask an inmate why he's here; it's always never his fault
Don't do the crime, don't do the time…oops, they got caught!

HOLLYWOOD STARS

Celebrities get lots of breaks
A lot of simple things are free
Out in public or making an appearance
It seems they never have to pay the fee

Hanging out in Beverly Hills or Hollywood
With all the lights and the glitz
Making millions from a career of acting
Living it up with their wealth and the ritz

They own million dollar mansions
Driven around in long lavish cars
Traveling the world at the drop of a hat
Always rubbing elbows with other famous stars

Unhappy when something doesn't go right
Let's see them live with less than $75,000 a year
After the big time they forget where they came from
Some not being down to earth, it's all crystal clear

They get their share for the life they live
Some of them being over rated
I guess that's the price of being a star
Pictures always taken and privacy invaded

Could they ever live a simple life?
Trading in their money and material things
When the last day comes they can't take it with them
While here on earth they are living like kings.

KEEPING ME GOING

When I think there is nothing left to write
One of my inspirations tells me not to lose sight
He reads my words and gives me his thought
Not knowing the reaction, I prepare for the assault

All he has read and not 1 negative comment yet
There are a few favorites that he won't forget
Looking at the future sometimes can be scary
To the one who motivates me, thank you Larry!

When I get in a slump and don't write a thing
His words to me are 'Don't you dare stop writing'
Putting on paper whatever comes to mind
Sometimes I make it to the middle, then I get in a bind

It's hard to write when the brain is froze
I sleep on it for a night, then I see how it goes
Most of my lines come with ease
When my head is unlocked by mental keys

A joy is brought to those that read
Letting the mind wander when my thoughts are freed
Running out of time, that's all I have for now
Don't worry there's more to come, thanks pal!

A HOSPITAL PATIENT

The hospital elevator travels between floors
Hundreds of patients a day go up and down
The sick and the injured enter through the doors
Admitted to stay, they're given a hospital gown

Some are there for surgery, others for major pain
Nurses are en-route to the patient's room
The psychiatric ward treats the insane
In Labor & Delivery, there's a child in the womb

The ambulance brings those in need of emergency attention
The O.R. is located on the floors above
At the top floor the elevator starts its dissention
The surgeons wash their hands then put on the glove

Some patients call in to the Patient Advisory Nurse
To ask questions about their medical condition
Those with serious problems get upset and even curse
Sometimes needing the advice of a physician

The morgue contains the bodies of the deceased
Patients needing to calm down are put under sedation
Once they are treated then they are released
Off to the Pharmacy to get their medication.

POLICE OFFICERS

In the realm of police work there is a lot of danger
Not always knowing what to expect
Out in public dealing with a stranger
On the crime scene its evidence they collect

On the roads, conducting a traffic stop
The citation is issued with the fines
Seldom allowing the penalty to drop
On the road of life you must stay inside the lines

Not a closed case until someone is arrested
It seems you're guilty until proven innocent
The case goes to trial where the charges are contested
Not all being the same, each case is different

Dressed up in the lawman's uniform
Driving their cruiser with radar and lights
With a call on the radio, the officers swarm
At the scene the subject is in their sights

To protect and serve is a rule that they follow
Trying to make a difference where they can
Negativity & destruction is sometimes hard to swallow
Preventing crime on the streets is the officer's plan.

SNOWY WINTER FUN

Around the neighborhood the weather turns cold
For now, summer activities are put on hold
On an overcast day the snow starts to fall
Time to go outside and make a snowball

The state will cancel school for the day
The kids dress warm and go out to play
Some make snowmen; others ride their sled
Still others would rather play in the woods instead

Half the day gone, clothes & gloves are soaking wet
Snow still falling, the next day's plans are set
Night falls and everyone heads for the big hill
The best sledding in town where everyone gets a thrill

On top of the hill is a bright warm fire
People up there half the night, not wanting to retire
Bored with the sleds, we throw snowballs at a truck
Getting into mischief, the teenagers have run amuck

Some people in the vehicles stop and give chase
The kids scatter into their favorite hiding place
After a few moments the children return again
Running from the cops so we won't end up in 'The Pen'

A few days pass and the snow melts away
The fun is over until the next snowy day
Now grown up, other youth have taken our spot
That was our winter fun until the days got hot.

HIGH SPEED CHASE

The speeding cars race through the street
As police chase a person who broke the law
Seeing the lights and hearing the sirens
Public safety in jeopardy, there's no room for flaw

While cruisers follow on the ground
A helicopter has the eye in the sky
Searching for a place they will never be found
Wishing for the officers to pass them by

Reacting in the heat of the moment
The driver runs through everything in sight
Striking other cars, objects, and people
For some innocent citizens, the outcome is a fright

Having disregard for those around them
The fleeing offender throws caution to the wind
After crashing the car, many flee on foot
As police subdue the subject, to the ground they are pinned

Innocent people get caught in the middle
As the dangerous driver speeds down the road
At the termination of many of these chases
There is broken bodies and wreckage to be towed

It doesn't pay to run from the law
The call on the radio cannot be escaped
With no govt. law for chase procedures
Rules for the high-speed chase need to be shaped.

GOSSIP

Facing adversity in your days
Don't let it hold you down
The gossiping people don't know what to say
When there is a new person in town

People will always tell stories
Not all of them always being true
Always needing something to talk about
With some stories, it's trouble they brew

Boring lives consist of nonsense
Having too much time on their hands
The rumors are spread through false words
In many cultures and in many lands

These types are with an unproductive life
It seems they need a little ambition
Some being the 'upper class' of society
Talking about things that are sometimes fiction

It makes it better for everyone
When all the rumors are put to rest
Those guilty should worry about themselves
To avoid being the next person's pest.

CONTROL FREAK

A need to dictate what another person does
Imposing their will, telling others what to do
They are addicted to the feeling of being in control
In a team environment, they're a 1-man crew

Trying to make and enforce all the rules
Adding resentment and making others rebel
In their own eyes & mind they think nothing is wrong
Attempting to convince those involved that all is well

They should take themselves out of the equation
Watch from the sidelines and loosen their grip
For the control freak that would never work
This type of action would destroy their power trip

Get input from others on what's happening
Some people are afraid of a change
Working with others would be more tolerable
Stepping away from the power, the controller feels strange

Put the ball in another person's hands
Give someone else the opportunity and the chance
With the end product, those in charge may be impressed
As they open their eyes and mind and take a 2nd glance.

UNSAFE DRIVERS

People trying to do 2 things at once
Talking on the cell phone while attempting to drive
Too many times they are the cause of an accident
Unfortunately, there are some that don't survive

Operating a vehicle is a 'full time job'
Requiring all concentration and skill
Comfortable drivers get complacent behind the wheel
Then there are the wild ones who drive for a thrill

Driving today is different from the old days
Vehicle operators on the roads have increased
On the street now it's a matter of life and death
Roads across the world are the place of many deceased

A lot of times the cause is operator error
Making bad decisions while driving their car
You see every day those who cannot drive safely
This includes the people who are leaving the bar

Advice to these drivers is plain and simple
Stay off the phone and pay attention to the road
Make the streets safer for everyone around you
Otherwise, one day it may be your car that is towed.

CHAPTER VIII – MISC. POEMS

VACATION TO GERMANY

The countryside of Germany is pretty in the spring
If you have the time and cash, visit if you get the chance
Everywhere you look there will be beautiful fields
One of the countries it borders is France

Each of the towns are separated by fields
Anything you may need is near
The distance between is 10 to 15 kilometers
Many have their own brewery and beer

Germany has a coastline and big cities
The capitol being called Berlin
Traveling east to the edge of Bavaria
The salt mines are located that you can fall in

The mines produce a large amount of Germany's salt
In the fields will be found barley and wheat
For the brewing of the beer and feeding of the sheep
A vacation in this country is quite a treat

Berlin is like New York; the cities that never sleep
You can always find something to do
A few other cities are Heidelberg and Cologne
Around the country there are many castles to view

The city of Koln has a very large cathedral
One of the biggest in the land
The Walt Disney castle originated in Neuschwanstein
On the beach there will be castles of sand

Now travel to Berchesgaden in the Alps
Here the Kelsteinhaus is perched up high
Known to Americans as the Eagles Nest
The view from the balcony of this building will make you say
'Oh my!'

Within this country there is much history
Air-raid shelters and death camps from Hitler's war
Gas chambers and human ash piles from the ovens
Mark the genocide that make human's feelings sore

There are holidays and many 'fests'
The only need for a party is a reason
Much beer is drank and much food is eaten
The main being Oktoberfest takes place in the fall season.

SR-71 BAND

It started one day about 16 years ago
Together with some friends, we went to see a band
Back then they were called 'Honor Among Thieves'
Front and center of the stage is were we stand

Every time they played we were sure to attend
Hammerjack's, The Paragon, or Network was the place
A group of college guys on stage having fun
Writing original music, their limit is outer space

After 1 CD, the band dismantled
Each member going their separate way
One member keeps moving forward
He will live to sing another day

After a long time, he is doing well today
With a new group of guys, I think he's got the nitch
Playing & singing with a band called SR-71
The talented front-man is known as Mitch

Along side of the time-keeper from Child's Play
Allan & Allen (Mitch & John) are quite the team
Working on a 4th CD and opening the Gravity Games
Putting together music that flows like a stream

Keep writing the good music
The only direction to go is ahead
The band SR-71 and the front-man Mitch Allan
A band with much potential, I think that's 'nuff said!

PULSE/ 1994

Bright lights shining in time
Millions go to work, but don't have a dime.
A dramatic display of talent, I wish I were there
A beautiful voice is heard from a face with blonde hair.

Music with meaning makes me think of my friend
It would be nice for 1 more tour before their end.
Sitting here with a brew, enjoying the sound
Hoping they will come for 1 more round.

Lights fall bringing back memories from the past
A time I don't want to forget and thoughts that will always
last.
Hard working people, now the leaf falls
Those who have a will and try have my applause.

My favorite song now they play
The words of my far away friend, I remember what they say
Watching the show, I'm happy and sad at the same time
I felt the need to sit and write this rhyme.

Every light is shining; every gimmick is at the end
All the happy thoughts, I long to relive again.
Now we're at the end and the great star explodes
Still thinking of the past, there are many future episodes.

In the year 1994 is when it was made
Sometime in 2004 is when I wish it was played.
Sometimes so serene like a still lake,
When I left Europe; A piece of my soul it did take.

I know my buddy's songs; Crazy Diamond, Us & Them
It seems impossible to get ahead in today's system.
It's kind of like elevator music but with an attitude
Search the depths of your mind, Do you ride on my
wavelength dude?

A crowd at Earl's Court of many sisters & brothers
The guitar player is good; but like many others.
The laser light is bright, like looking into the sun
When I'm done with this poem, I'm sure there will be another
one.

My friend in a land far away; His words I wish to hear
I wish he lived a little closer then we could share a beer.
I don't understand the whole movie, It makes me wonder
If the musicians fell off their pedestal it would be a great
blunder.

Two of my favorites; Take it Back & Run Like Hell
Will my wheels ever stop turning? Only time will tell.
The lights are like something from the 4th of July
Every poem comes from the heart; I just let my mind fly!

This show I've seen so many times
I'm thankful where I am today despite all my crimes
What's wrong with the world today? Is everything money &
greed?
Can't anyone be humble and settle for what they need?

Sometimes I try to get people thinking with the words I write
If you do understand maybe you will see some of my light.
It's not hard to do, all you need to do is think
If you don't then maybe all you see is one shade of pink.

The plane comes crashing; That's the end of it all
Before the 21st century we brought down 'The Wall'
When I grew up you never heard of guns in school
Now-a-days kids think this crap is cool.

He points to the crowd, now it's your turn to feel the heat
Once you've seen the light, isn't that neat?
The sound is loud, kind of like a scream
Like a locomotive letting off lots of steam.

Now is the time I must go to bed
Later I'll write more of the dreams in my head.

POWER

Sitting after work hearing the sounds of the tune
Some of the lyrics have so much power,
Look out the window to the brightness of the moon
Now in my back yard there is one more flower

Like a semi- truck with the peddle to the floor
Singing words with so much force & feeling
Having a 'say-so' in the world and desiring more
The revenue of the middle class is what Washington is stealing

Having the motivation to do what needs to be done
Owning the determination to accomplish every goal
Playing a game you know you have won
Now for the price of success you pay the toll

Similar to a jet engine swamped with fuel
The force pushes the jet very fast
The radical Muslims are very cruel
In the very end, I wonder how many will last

Knowledge is power, the brain is a valuable tool
Move in one direction, that be forward; and don't look back
Like a pack of hungry wolves with mouths of drool
Under great pressure you will never crack.

MILITARY BASIC TRAINING

Army, Navy, Air Force, Marines
These are the armed forces of the United States
In boot camp every recruit cleans the latrines
A military power the rest of the world hates

Wake up early to go on a 2-mile run
They are always those that fall behind
Gasping for breath, they're glad they're done
Getting used to life of a different kind

After cleaning up, its off to the Mess Hall
Every new soldier feels worn out and tired
In the obstacle course they will be climbing 'The Wall'
The next day at the range, the M-16's will be fired

Each day they will learn how to march and sing
The intense physical activity never stops
As every day passes they will learn a new thing
Then back to the barracks where they utilize the mops

Time spent in the field, they learn the rules of war
Living outside in the wild
Getting in the vehicles, they hear the engines roar
Back to headquarters where the equipment is piled

After a couple of months the training is done
The recruits finally get to rest
Some soldiers hate it, others think it's fun
With training completed they have passed the test.

THINKING

Sitting here listening to my tunes
Thinking of Germany, the barracks, & the rooms.
In time of the past , longing to return
The longer it takes , you can feel it burn.

I would like to share with my wife
She would have the time of her life.
Never leaving her home land
A strange place she would like to stand.

Remembering my german freind,
I have not seen in a long time
I send him many E-mails , keeping in touch
The postage is not even a dime.

Not forgetting about Panama
And all the good times that were had
It would be nice to visit again someday
Time spent would not be sad

The picture of the mountains ,
That are burned in my mind
A piece of me is there
It feels like something left behind.

It's the music I hear that takes me to the past
My voyage around the world happened fairly fast
Now I'm stuck here, sitting in this big state
Thinking of when I will travel, pondering the date.

The places and cultures that were seen
From one place to another, many miles in between
These things from earlier life I miss
My time spent here trying to reminisce.

It's getting late so I think I'll go to bed
The eyelids are heavy, feeling like lead
Sweet dreams are waiting in my room,
The time I wake should be around noon.

THE MEMORY REMAINS

It's stuck in my head, it won't go away
I have the same thought day after day
When I see the things I have seen before
I think of the day when I will see them no more

I don't want this day to come, I'm not ready to fly
If I think about it too hard a tear will come to my eye
These thoughts flash through my head on days when it rains
No matter how hard I try to forget, the memory remains

First my mind is blank, then a flash of a past love
Then I picture myself laying in my bed and seeing her face
above
I remember these things any time of the day
I try to forget the thoughts but I know there is no way

The cycle keeps on happening week after week
I wish they would go away, it's solitude that I seek
I try so hard to clear out my brain
I realize now that the memories remain.

OCTOBER 31ST

October 31st is the day of Halloween
Kids dress up like a cartoon or a ghost
Walking the neighborhood after dark
Bags of candy is what children want most

Traveling the streets to every house
Soon comes a knock at the door
Spoken are the words "Trick or Treat"
Going to the next house in search of more

Costumes you see in almost every store
Also inside will be lots of candy
Houses are decorated in the spirit of the holiday
Using household articles & whatever is handy

It's a fun time for the children
Safety is the key word of the night
Throwing away anything looking suspicious
And anything that is not wrapped up tight

After all the sweets are gone
Seeing Santa Claus is next on the list
Hoping for lots of presents and gifts
A child's sense of wanting will always persist

Photos are taken of the children's costumes
From running and excitement they start to sweat
Having a good time and doing silly things
To cherish the times and never forget.

THE PRO WRESTLER

Gladiators of old performed in the coliseum
Today, the stage is known as a ring
A squared circle, measuring 20 ft. by 20 ft.
The battle is started by the bell that goes 'ding'

Two opponents start the contest
Not always knowing what the other will do
Executing acrobatic maneuvers and holds
The show put on by the performers & the crew

Dressed in nylon spandex suits
And many different colors of tights
With calf high boots and wrists wrapped of tape
Spectators are out for a night at the fights

The outcome of the match is pre-determined
Performed like a choreographed dance
Sometimes talking their way through it
The action looks real at a glance

The sport is accompanied by theater
Professionals that are good at their job
Many of them having muscular bodies
Looking like a modern day heart throb

With the right mix of character and charisma
With a high income, the athlete is being well paid
The rule of thumb 'The more you draw, the more you make'
For the love of their profession, many would not trade

When they get too old and the body gives out
They retire with names etched with fame
Giving their contribution to the industry they love
Professional wrestling is the name of their game.

THE RIDE

Going to your favorite amusement park
Lit up like a Christmas tree after dark
Getting on every roller coaster & exciting ride
Seeing many attractions with your map as your guide

Roller coaster rides can be a fun time
There are high-speed turns after a vertical climb
Disney World is a very popular park
On your next vacation, make it a mark

Riding Space Mountain, its difficult to see
Not knowing what's coming, suspense is the key
When the ride is over, the time was not a bore
After 2 or 3 times, you'll want to ride some more

Leaving Space for the next mountain of Splash
You can ride all day once you've paid the cash
A slow water ride that you may think is a flop
Until the end is reached with a 6 story drop

The newer ride of today don't go by rail
Powered by magnets & electric on a high speed trail
In search of the rides that are bigger and faster
People seeking the epitome with adrenaline as their master

Some attractions are dry and others are wet
Your fun being based on the excitement you get
The anticipation is so thick; you could cut it with a knife
After the fun is over its back to everyday life.

BALTIMORE AND VICINITY

In this city is the Inner Harbor
An attraction with lots of shops
Close to the Science Center & National Aquarium
Just 1 place to visit on the list of many stops

A building that used to be called 'The Power Plant'
Urban Legend says it was the city morgue
Around the city there are manufacturing buildings
Like the Domino Sugar Co. and a local brewery of Tuborg

Near the harbor is Oriole Park at Camden Yards
Not far away is a stadium for Ravens football
At Fells Point is the foundry of Bethlehem Steel
The city of Baltimore, Maryland has it all

About a 3 hour drive away is Ocean City
Located on the Eastern Shore there's a beach
Downtown you will find the city jail
And the university where the professors teach

Crossing the Chesapeake Bay is a tunnel & a bridge
On the eastern side are the lands for farming
In the western side are the Appalachian Mountains
When summer approaches, the weather starts warming

Bordering the states of Virginia and Pennsylvania
There is a lot of history around the state
Near the Potomac River is the District of Colombia
A little farther is Mount Vernon; George Washington's estate

In this area of the country there is much history
The land bearing the scars of the Civil War
The northern boundary being the Mason Dixon Line
At Ocean City is located the Atlantic shore

While traveling through this region
Be sure to see many of the sights
Not knowing if & when you will return
Knowledge of the area could take you to new heights.

APARTMENT LIFE

Near the apartments, people are all around
Searching for peace & quiet, rarely is it found
Tenants above and below, maybe on either side
Learning how to deal with it, taking it all in stride

Outside of the building is never dull
Rowdy children are shouting in the hall
All day long the kids run and play
Hearing noise half the night in bed where you lay

Walking to the stores and shops in a short time
People close together, there's more tendency for crime
Standing on the corner, waiting on the bus for school
When the kids get home, its off for a swim at the pool

Always something to do, friends many times are nearby
Getting into mischief, idle time is the reason why
Finding something constructive is not always hard to do
Choosing the friends that like to do the same things as you

Throughout the complex, you may see cops once or twice
When the snow hits, you make money shoveling snow and ice
Once grown up, many people go their separate ways
For some families, the apartments are where they spend all of
their days.

THE FIRST INNING

A Sunday outing at the local stadium
Arriving early to find a place to park
Buying a ticket in your section of choice
The light will fade and soon will be dark

Now it's game time, the teams take to the field
Then comes the ceremonial first pitch
Out of a dugout full of players comes the 1st batter
In the batter's box with his foot he digs a small ditch

The pitch comes to the catcher at home plate
Was it a strike or was it a ball?
Sometimes the players and crowd get irate
Because of the umpire that made a bad call

A player gets a hit and is now on base
Waiting to cross the plate for a score
Another player is up and hits a home run
Turning one run into 3 or even 4

Soon the inning will be over
After 3 outs the teams trade places
It's up to this team to get the runs in
As the batters get hits and round the bases

After 9 innings usually is a winner
In the news interview we'll hear what they say
It may be at home or in another city
The game is over until the next one they play.

AN URBAN LEGEND

A long dark road winding through the trees
To a paper recycling co. at the bottom of the hill
A train trestle going across the river
The fog rolls in with the air being still

Not far away is the insane asylum
An abandoned hospital for the mentally sick
On the top of the hill is a creepy cemetery
Driving on the road is dangerous because it is slick

The place is known as 7 hills
There are really only 5 in all
How it got its name, I don't know
A spooky place to be where the trees are tall

In another part of the woods is a satanic church
The place is empty with nothing inside
Graves from the 1800's freshly dug in the yard
A place with an evil aura that makes you want to hide

The door is locked and every window is barred
Such a blood curdling, creepy, dark place
A building in which no sane person would worship
A congregation bound together by an evil embrace

Going under what's called Crybaby Bridge
Urban legend says a baby died here
Listen very closely and the sound can be heard
Hearing the sounds, the heart is filled with fear

Sitting under the bridge in your car
On the windshield will appear drops
Of what some say is the child's blood
On either side of the road is a field full of crops

Seeing these places with a group of friends
A place you would never go to alone
Not going empty handed; a few had a gun
The stories of this place are chilling to the bone

The images are burnt into my memory
Of these places I will never forget
How many others have seen what I have?
Not thinking I'm the last, on that you can bet.

THE DARK UNKNOWN

The witching hour is close at hand
In this age, evil plots are planned
On the television are shows about ghosts
Broadcasted on networks from coast to coast

Some of these issues go on unexplained
Trying to be proven by people that are trained
The darkness can be felt within the air
With anything possible, is there something there?

Studying the paranormal and strange things
No questions answered with the mystery it brings
After crossing over, is it possible to come back?
A case that science is wanting to crack

Illinois is where many of the stories originate
In the Chicago area, the chances here are great
People see things they have no explanation for
Maybe here is a spot for another dimension's door

Resurrection Mary being seen by more than one at night
A woman on the roadside always wearing white
Headed toward a place called something like Arrowhead Lane
People that meet her, are they mentally stable & sane?

Shrouded in mystery, there are no answers in sight
The unknown being a brain twisting fright
So far, there are no stories of anyone harmed
Just strange happenings that keep people alarmed.

THE DAY BEFORE CHRISTMAS

T'was the day before Christmas
And all through the town
The disgruntled last minute shoppers
Standing in the checkout line with a frown

Rushing through department stores
Purchasing that last needed present
Hurrying home with much wrapping to do
So the family and in-laws will all be pleasant

The decorations are all hung
Around every part of the house
Tearing open the wrapping
Of a present from your spouse

Getting ready for the company
Making sure the food is just right
There is difficulty with unwrapping the gifts
Some are wrapped up way too tight

Assembly needed for many of the toys
Batteries required for almost every one
Running around all week long
After this night it will all be done

Now is the time for a photo opportunity
Camera flashes come from every side
Catching some in unwanted positions
Running from the camera, they try to hide

The children are headed outdoors
To take a ride on their new bike
They want to play with everything at once
Not figuring out which one they really like

After the big day is over
Everything is stored for the next year
Having a repeat of the past week
To some people is their biggest fear

When all is said and done
It wasn't such a bad time
Except for the maxed out credit bills
Where you will spend every hard earned dime.

A DESTRUCTIVE FIRE

Wood burning in the fireplace
Radiating heat throughout the room
Heat too close to combustible items
Could cause the house to go Ka'Boom

Homes made mostly of wood
Quickly the fire is able to spread
Flames engulf and char the structure
Battled by people on a truck of red

Too many times the house is not empty
Someone in the building has died
Sometimes with no smoke detectors installed
Not able to escape, they are trapped inside

The house that once was, is no more
Flames have turned the wood to ash
On this spot needing to be rebuilt
First must be removed all of the trash

Burning down the forested land
Trees and plants are now a pile of coals
Happening at any time and place
Between the north and south poles

Fire can be useful and friendly
If unmanaged, it will burn out of control
Consuming everything in its path
If not stopped, it will take its toll

Anytime you are dealing with a fire
Take precautions and handle with care
It only takes a spark to get something going
Anyone around these situations should Beware!

A MYSTICAL PATH

A walk through the woods on a cool damp night
A heavy fog sets in through the trees
Opening your ear to the sounds of nature
The air being still with no hint of a breeze

Traveling down a dimly lit path
Noise is reduced with leaves on the ground
During the stroll a covered bridge appears
Underneath the crossing water is found

Watching the water flow downstream
The tributary empties into the lake
White vapor rises up off of the surface
When daylight arrives the forest will awake

Along the journey through the medieval land
Stands a castle constructed of stone
Perched on the top of a hill
On its walls moss and ivy have grown

Things seem creepy in the misty woods
With one not knowing what to expect
Many get nervous when it comes to the unknown
Afraid of something that the senses don't detect

Making it back to the starting point
The nights' journey is terminated by the light
Daybreak emerges to a mystical morning
Once the fog burns off the day will become bright.

DEMON ALCOHOL

Demon alcohol
Makes the vision blur
Demon alcohol
Makes your stomach stir

Demon alcohol
Too much will make you sick
Demon alcohol
Causes the brain not to tick

Demon alcohol
Slows reaction time
Demon alcohol
Can take you out of your prime

Demon alcohol
Is able to screw up your life
Demon alcohol
Like cold butter to a hot knife

Demon alcohol
Always drinking more than you should
Demon alcohol
Does the human body no good

Demon alcohol
Hitting rock bottom isn't very fun
Demon alcohol
Hangover sets in when you're finally done

Demon alcohol
Listen to what is said
Demon alcohol
The dependency is in your head
Demon alcohol
Quit now before you're dead!

FOOTBALL GAME

A Sunday afternoon at the stadium
Where there is a football game to be played
Parking and entrance is granted
With the possession of a ticket that is paid

Once inside the facility
Your destination is to your seat
Heading down to the 1st row
Where there are players to meet & greet

The opening kickoff takes place
The game is now underway
Players are lying all over the field
After being tackled they are all okay

Two teams battle for a 15-minute period
There are 4 of these in all
An attempted pass is intercepted
Now the other team has the ball

Many teams compete on the gridiron
All striving for 1st place
The top teams make it to the playoffs
While trying to keep up with the pace

The best 2 teams go to the championship game
Better known as the Super Bowl
The excitement builds as the end is near
This championship is won by a 3-point field goal.

VIOLENCE IN SPORTS

The recent years of professional sports
What's wrong with the players of today?
Violent confrontations between teams
Athletes can't conduct themselves in a professional way

Unless physical provocation takes place
Players should never enter the stands
Spectators not safe and lawsuits can be filed
Innocent fans could get hurt by someone else's hands

Too many times the players get away
Because of all the money that they make
They should be made to face the repercussions
Of their actions that put people's safety at stake

These people are no different than you or I
We all put on our pants the same way
They should quit fighting & concentrate on the game
After all, don't they get paid to play?

Baseball, basketball, and all other sports
Players that misbehave should be heavily fined
What kind of message is being sent to the young?
Behavior in pro sports needs to be redefined.

LACK OF SECURITY

Located at the entrance of the plant
The driver tries to enter but can't
Inside the fence sits the guard shack
The guard tells the driver to go around back

With this driver, the guards have a bad rap
The reason he's here is to pick up some scrap
Security sends him to the wrong door
Sitting for over an hour, the man was sore

His point of contact works on the other side
Saying security sent him here; I guess they lied
This was not the first time, it's happened before
As he leaves the gate you can hear the truck roar

Here is another driver with a delivery up the street
What is security telling all these truckers they meet?
If this industry was high tech., problems could arise
The wrong person entering could be the company's demise

At their job, the security guards need to improve
If they can't get it right maybe they should move
Out of this job and into another profession
Because safety is this company's biggest obsession.

MOTIVATION & SUCCESS

From the very first day
With the first drawn breath
Until the very last day
When the body approaches death

There are those people that wonder
What their life's purpose is here
The storm of life sets in; there is a sound of thunder
Hindsight is 20/20, now all is seen clear

Children develop aspirations when they are young
Each one choosing a different profession
Climbing the ladder of success rung by rung
Learning from failure, not falling into depression

Motivated ones strive to do their best
Staring into the face of adversity
Utilizing talents and putting their skills to the test
Taught in every school and university

Success achieved by the hard work done
Passing their knowledge to others when they can
Given the opportunity to pick up the ball and run
No two lives being the same, each has a different plan

There are sometimes those that make a bad decision
Not always choosing the best way to go
Running on the right path like a man on a mission
Overcoming any obstacle, always refusing to slow

As the latter part of life draws near
Giving back that which they have received
Leaving a legacy to others still here
Many things accomplished, because in themselves, they
believed

Lesson:
 Believe in yourself and always put your heart & soul into
anything you do.......success will come!

Inspired by lyrics written by Tamyra Gray
Recorded by Diana DeGarmo

THE UNBELIEVING

People sometimes laugh when you try your best
When putting forth effort, putting your skills to the test
Believe in yourself and never refuse to try
At the end of the night, watching the others sigh

The outcome is not always as you want it to be
On the losing team, victory you long to see
On the stage of life, you always want to be #1
Whether accepted or not, the object is to have fun

Singing or dancing, the effort is all your own
Looking at day one, your progression has grown
Entered in a contest and sometimes you may win
If not meant to be, look at your strengths within

In the game of life, you always want to be on top
Your progression seems to slow, don't ever stop
When on the highest cliff, the only direction is to drop
Striving to reach the pinnacle, nobody desires to flop

The performer wants every ticket to sell
If the majority are gone he may say 'oh well!'
Your end plan may never come to be
But you have the chance in the land of the free!

THE YEARS' END

The air outside is starting to get cold
The beginning of a new year is about to unfold
Dress for the weather or your body will freeze
People get sick as they cough, sniffle, and sneeze

The holiday season is now at hand
The hustle & bustle is more than some can stand
This is a happy and joyous time of the year
As heavy snow falls, visibility isn't always clear

Time to make plans for the year that will come
Making the plans reality is hard for many but easier for some
As the year comes to a close, another will begin
With the holidays over, people try to stay thin

Eager for a new year as the old one winds down
Many parties are happening all over town
It's out with the old and in with the new
People continue to do what they always do

Hoping the next year is better than the last
Changing some things that were done in years past
It seems the older you get, the faster time flies
A new day is started when the sun begins to rise.

NEW YEARS DAY

The city is quiet on New Years Day
A new beginning as the old year fades away
Time to make that promise that we seldom keep
Forgetting the resolutions after falling fast asleep

The 1st of the year brings a new start on the way
Changing the things that are in disarray
Making an effort to make this year better than the last
Recalling different things in many years past

Progressing through life, moving straight ahead
Striving to go forward but falling backwards instead
Will the end of this year be like the one before?
We'll have to see what the future has in store

As the months go by, your age increases by one
Engaging in activities that make this year fun
At the end of this year, it's a night out on the town
At midnight in Times Square, another year is down

As the ball drops, parties are well under way
After 12:01am, for 24 hours it is New Years Day
When the day is over the New Year will begin
At this point in time, the old year has shed its skin.

TO THE READERS OF THIS BOOK

In your busy lives you will come and go
In whatever direction like the winds that blow
With new experiences, knowledge is gained
With every black mark, perfect lives are stained

As your days pass by, remember one thing
Treat others the way you want them to treat you
Anger and frustration can be easily managed
By putting yourself in the other person's shoe

In every day of your life, try to do what is right
If everyone did this, the world would be a better place
Unfortunately, you have to take the good with the bad
Until we cease to exist as a human race

With the mountain of life ahead of you to climb
I want to thank you all for taking the time
For opening the cover and having a look
I hope you enjoyed the stories in this book

Thank You,
Best Wishes and God Bless You!

Printed in the United States
71225LV00005B/157-165

9 781425 965563